SPODE'S
WILLOW PATTERN
& other designs after the Chinese

SPODE'S
WILLOW PATTERN
& other designs after the Chinese
ROBERT COPELAND

STUDIO VISTA/CHRISTIE'S

A Studio Vista/Christie's book published
by Cassell Ltd,
35 Red Lion Square, London, WC1R 4SG
an affiliate of
Macmillan Publishing Co., Inc., New York

Copyright © Robert Copeland 1980

First published in 1980

ISBN 0 289 70893 1

Designed by Roger Davies
Phototypeset by TNR Productions London
Printed by Morrison and Gibb, Ltd.

TO THE MEMORY OF MY FATHER
GRESHAM COPELAND
who taught me so much
and kindled my interest
in blue and white

Foreword and acknowledgements

My first debt of gratitude is to my wife whose fore-bearance while I worked on this book enabled me to complete it, and my daughter Emma for her help. Next to my many colleagues and friends at Spode Limited who as collectors or craftsmen have advised and helped me in very many ways: Harold Holdway and his son, Paul, Philip Plant, Jack Amos for printing the transfers from old Spode engravings and Keith Borrell his supervisor, Jean Bettaney, the late Sam Williams and Paul Thorpe for their help in tracing patterns, Carol Reading for typing the manuscript, and my fellow Directors for granting me unrestricted access to any material I needed.

Many friends have allowed me to photograph objects in their collections or have provided photographs: Rosemary and Rustom Patel, Minnie Holdway, Frank Rabone and his friends, Henry Irvine-Fortescue, Martin Pulver, Alan Willis, Pat Latham, Cyril Williams-Wood, Jack Palfrey, Geoffrey Godden, John and Una des Fontaines, Alan Smith, Dean Rockwell, David Allen, and several others. Messrs. Sotheby Parke Bernet and the City of Liverpool Museums have also been most helpful.

In researching the subjects my task would have been impossible without the considerable help of J.S. McNally, Helen Proudlove, Derek Beard and his staff at the Hanley Reference Library, and on specific subjects Susan Hare at Goldsmiths Hall, Geoffrey de Bellaigue, Messrs. Christie, Manson & Woods, Philip Smyrk of Johnson Matthey, Philip Miller, Maurice Procter and John Shaw of Blythe Colours Ltd, Roy Taylor of Ramsden's Ltd, John Collins, Kai Hunstadbraten of Modum, Norway and Dr. Eiler Schiotz, John and Felicity Mallet, Colin Wyman, Reginald Haggar, Elizabeth Heatherington and Lynne Sussman of Parks Canada, Henry Sandon, Bernard Watney, Elizabeth Collard, Paul Atterbury, David Howard, H.A. Crosby Forbes, John Austin, Arnold Mountford, John Bellak, and Alison Griffin who photographed Paul Holdway reproducing the bat printing process.

To Leonard Whiter, whose book *Spode* is my constant companion and guide, I record my appreciation for his advice and the sense of direction his previous work has given to this study. I would also like to thank Anthony Brindley and the staff of Moorland Photolabs Limited for their help with the photography, Norman Jones for the colour photography, and Roger Davies and Conway Lloyd Morgan for the design and editorial work.

Lastly, to Arlene Palmer, Curatorial Assistant at the Henry Francis du Pont Museum, Winterthur, for reading the manuscript and making innumerable constructive suggestions for its improvement, I acknowledge my deepest appreciation.

ROBERT COPELAND

Contents

The colour plates are between pages 78 and 79.

Introduction

Blue and white ceramics have long held the eye of the collector. Near Eastern potters first used cobalt oxide as a blue colourant, but it was the Chinese porcelains decorated with cobalt that popularized the taste for blue and white in the West. Of the millions of Chinese porcelains exported to Europe and America between 1600 and 1900, the vast majority were painted with designs in blue.

The oriental landscapes and genre scenes of China trade porcelains greatly influenced the English earthenware industry of the late eighteenth and early nineteenth centuries. Potters in Staffordshire and elsewhere copied Chinese motifs directly or developed oriental themes of their own. These designs were sometimes painted but more often were applied by the technique of transfer-printing.

More than any other English potter, Josiah Spode responded to the influence of the Chinese. Because many of the blue and white oriental patterns the Spode firm marketed were also produced by other manufacturers, the attribution of individual objects in these designs has been very difficult for the collector.

Robert Copeland's detailed analysis of blue transfer-printed earthenware in the oriental style is based on documented examples from Spode and other factories. The author has also drawn upon the evidence of engraved copper plates that survive at Spode. Patterns and their variants are illustrated and fully described, and Copeland's system of classification will encourage a standard terminology. The book will undoubtedly prove an invaluable guide for collectors of English blue and white, clarifying many of the attribution problems in this field.

Robert Copeland has had a long association with Spode. His experience on the factory has enabled him to produce a work that is rich in technical detail concerning the use of cobalt and the process of transfer-printing. He has placed his subject within the broader contexts of 'china mania' and the British pottery industry, making this a delightful, as well as informative, study.

ARLENE M. PALMER
The Henry Francis du Pont Winterthur Museum

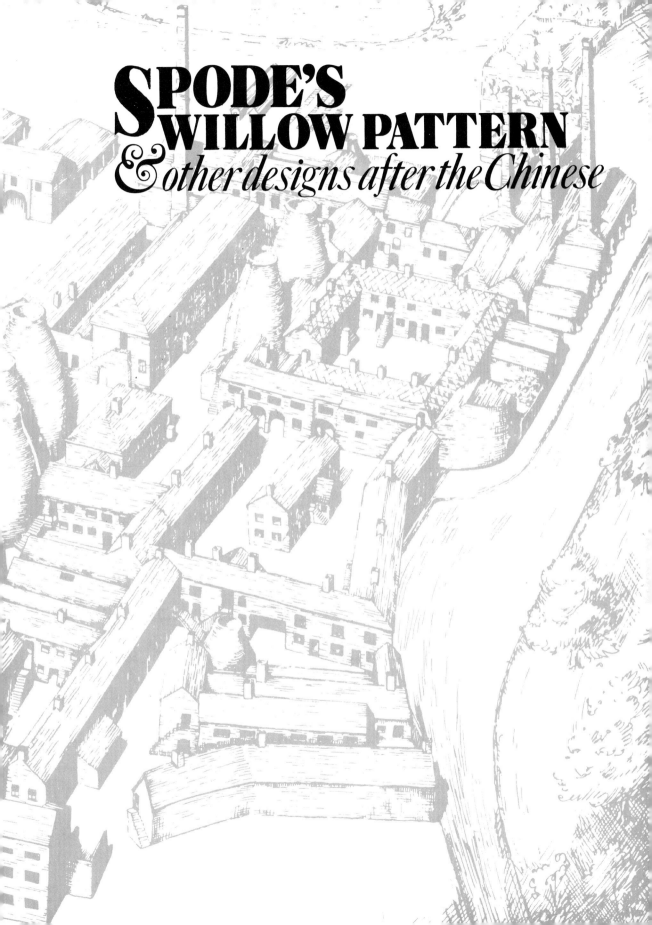

SPODE'S
WILLOW PATTERN
& other designs after the Chinese

Mr Copeland and Mr Spode signing their partnership agreement.

1 History
of the period 1770 - 1803

JOSIAH SPODE responded more than any other English potter to the influence of Chinese export porcelain. This chapter examines some of the external factors which affected the pottery trade in Britain, and those events which presented opportunities that were grasped by Spode in particular.

The rise of the Staffordshire Potteries was due to the rich deposits of coal which outcropped at the surface adjacent to the excellent red clays[32]. By 1660 a small industry was becoming established and soon, by concentrating on manufacturing and selling their products to itinerant pot-sellers, or cratemen, the potters developed North Staffordshire as the British centre for pottery making. The aim of the more ambitious potters, to discover the secret of making white pottery, led to the invention of tin-glazed earthenware, while in Staffordshire the earliest response to the challenge was to apply a slip of white-burning clay to a redware body; this was in 1723. Thus Josiah Spode I was born at a time when the English manufacturers were developing many new ceramic bodies, production techniques and commercial enterprises.

For example, Enoch Booth is credited with introducing a new method of glazing in about 1740 [172], by which the fired clayware, or 'biscuit', is immersed or 'dipped', into a fluid suspension of lead-based glass materials in water, called 'glaze'. This was then re-fired at a lower temperature. It was realised that decorations could be painted onto the biscuit ware and sealed under the glaze. As far as is known, only cobalt blue was used in this way during the eighteenth century.

The completion of the Grand Trunk Canal in 1777, linking the River Trent at Wilden Ferry with the Mersey at Runcorn Gap, meant that raw materials such as flints, clays, and Cornish stone could be transported more cheaply to the Potteries, and also provided an ideal route for the export of pottery from Staffordshire, either to North America via Liverpool or to Europe via Hull[32]. Two years earlier, in 1775, the potters of Staffordshire, led by Josiah Wedgwood, had campaigned successfully against Richard Champion's monopoly on the use of china clay and Cornish stone[1].

As to the market for the potters' wares, in the mid-eighteenth century the dinnerware used by most wealthy people was Chinese porcelain, imported in huge quantity by the Honourable East India Company[130]. The very rich might dine off silver, or the humblest off pewter. In the years between 1740 and 1770 Staffordshire white salt-glazed stoneware enjoyed a certain popularity, reaching a zenith in about 1760, when English tin-glazed earthenware also reached its peak. Indeed salt-glazed ware continued to be made until the end of the century: Samuel Spode of the Foley, the second son of Josiah Spode I, is believed to have continued making the ware until the start of the nineteenth century[84].

By 1770, however, cream-coloured earthenware had proved its superiority over artificial or soft paste porcelains for dinner ware. While the porcelain manufacturers had considerable success with small items, teawares and dessert wares for example, they were quite unable to make large plates or platters[190]. Taste was changing in favour of creamware also. Its warm, cheerful and smart designs seemed ideal to complement the Neo-classical style of interior designers such as Adam and cabinet makers such as Sheraton. Josiah Wedgwood is justly praised for his perseverance in conducting trials to achieve a really satisfactory creamware. 1762 saw the result[187]: Her Majesty Queen Charlotte ordered 'a complete set of tea things'[46] of this creamware in June 1765, and later permitted Wedgwood to call it 'Queensware'[174].

The bestowing of this accolade brought Wedgwood, and other manufacturers of creamwares, considerable trade from the wealthy classes, to such an extent that Wedgwood was unable to manufacture sufficient ware to meet it. So it seems probable that local potters[45] supplied him with finished ware made according to his specification and often stored by them in their own warehouses. Reference[123] is made in a letter dated 13 March 1765 to Mr John Wedgwood, Cateaton Street, London, in which he refers to ware which has been packed from two neighbouring 'banks', those of Baddeley and Edge. It may well be that from this use of the word 'banks' the local Staffordshire term 'pot bank' came to mean a pottery manufactory[173].

The popularity of the Neoclassical style coupled with the availability of creamware affected the sales of Chinese porcelain dinnerware. But there was still a demand in the 1780s and 1790s for Chinese style designs, especially blue and white wares, from the professional and merchant classes. What the nobility found acceptable yesterday, the next lower level of society favours today. Probably some of the Chinese services were discarded in favour of creamware, and were acquired by others.

The first manufacturer to reproduce Chinese landscape patterns by blue printing was Caughley, near Broseley in Shropshire. This was on porcelain, not earthenware, and restricted at least initially to teawares. Blue decoration on creamware does not look right as the blue colour appears odd against the yellowish ground. So a new product was developed, which came to be known as pearlware. This was a pale ivory earthenware much the same as creamware, except that the glaze was stained with a small amount of cobalt to give a whiter appearance. This change cleared the ground for the adaptations of Chinese patterns, and these began to appear from Staffordshire and elsewhere.

The development of the Staffordshire potteries' competition with imported Chinese ware is bound up with the affairs of the Honourable East India Company, affairs in turn affected by political changes as well as the fortunes of trade.[22]The traditional route to China from Europe was by way of the Cape of Good Hope and thence either by India or the Indonesian islands. After a lengthy stay at Canton, where the ships anchored off Whampoa Island, and were laden with all kinds of commodities such as tea, lacquer, silks, ivories and spices, the return voyage would begin. The round trip from England could well occupy up to twenty-two months. Until the 1760s the East India Company, and their officers, trading privately, were importing huge quantities of blue and white porcelain into England for so little cost that the retail price was probably lower than for creamware. The cheap cost of labour in China both for potters and coolies explains the low price charged at Canton.[130]And in the cost of sea transport home another big saving was made. On the return voyage to England the ships usually met with heavy seas when water would seep into the hulls as the timbers moved. Porcelain was an ideal cargo to place in the wet bottoms of ships because it did not suffer from prolonged soaking in sea water.[180]It was packed in specially made, standardised wooden boxes which were placed in the bottom of the holds over the ballast to form a platform for other cargo.[134](See fig. 1) Officers were entitled to stow private cargo in this space also - the allocation depending on rank.[I]

Morse[127]quotes various accounts, for example, 'the china ware for flooring the ships, 300 chests in all, had been ordered in the winter' and 'of china ware each ship received, on Company's account, a general run of fifty chests and half chests, invoiced at Taels[II]1,200 to Taels 1,800 each ship: these went in first, directly over the kintledge and dunnage[III]to serve as flooring for the Bohea which went in the lowest tiers of tea.'[128]So the manner of loading was to put chinaware at the bottom, Bohea tea next above that, then Singlo and other fine teas, with the silk last.[129](See fig. 2)

Apart from the inevitable breakages, much chinaware arrived in an unsaleable condition, for sets were frequently found to consist of pieces of different patterns. Such losses on the Company's part seem to have been tolerated because of the profits on tea,[119]and perhaps because the supply of suitable vessels for drinking tea could only increase sales. Imported Chinese porcelain was sold at about two to four times the price paid in Canton, so that little or nothing of the freight cost was recovered. The introduction of creamware challenged the primacy of Chinese wares, and the assured market of the 1750s began to decline in later decades, as English manufacturers strove to perfect their own porcelains.

The Napoleonic Wars also had an impact on the

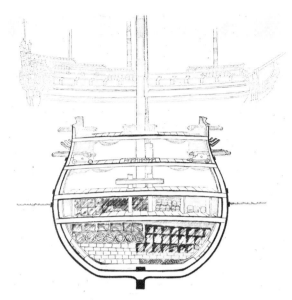

1. Drawing of an East Indiaman showing the arrangement of goods in the hold.

import of China trade porcelain, because of the high rate of duty imposed.[IV]The import duty on chinaware in 1787 was 47½ per cent,[23] but by 1799 it had been raised to £109.8.6d 'for every £100 of the true and real value thereof'. The American War of Independence had a further effect. After the signing of the Treaty of Versailles in 1783, American ship owners decided to trade directly with Canton, to reduce their dependence on Britain for imported Chinese goods, including porcelain. On 22 February 1784,[105]the first American ship, the *Empress of China*, left New York for Canton, thus beginning a trade that was over the next thirty to forty years to supply practically every household within reach of the Atlantic seaboard with all the Chinese porcelain it desired.[165]But by the end of the eighteenth century, English-made blue transfer-printed porcelain and earthenware had begun to arrive.

The Honourable East India Company ceased to import porcelain on its own account from the end of the 1798 trading season. Their own sale proceeds had dropped from £23,630 in 1763 to £7,332 in 1796. Even this latter figure covered a loss of £3,933. Over the period the volume of private trade seems to have dropped from £49,351 in 1763 to £1,613 in 1796. But it was not quite a case of a battle lost, for if less porcelain was

imported, it was to allow more space for importing tea.[V]

Tea was first introduced into England in 1650,[184] and the first recorded advertisement for it appeared in *Mercurius Politicus* in September 1658,[52]where it states 'that excellent, and by all physicians approved, China drink, called by the Chineans, Tcha, by other nations Tay alias Tee, is sold at the Sultaness-Head, a Cophee-house in Sweetings Rents by the Royal Exchange, London.' Tea remained a luxury for many years,[144]while the duty on it caused considerable annoyance to the English, and, as every schoolboy knows, the colonists of America!

In 1779 an Act of Parliament was passed to prohibit tea smuggling.[VI]In the same year, William Richardson, a director of the Honourable East India Company, published a pamphlet in which he condemned smuggling and the adulteration of tea. In it he alleged that the greater part of the imports into the other European countries was being smuggled into England.[138]The cost of the American War had caused the British Government to increase the duty on tea from 64 per cent in 1773 (the time of the Boston Tea Party) to 119 per cent on the auction value of all teas in

2. **Painted Tea Chest.** *Courtesy the Henry du Pont Winterthur Museum.*

1784.[53]Home consumption of duty-paid tea was about five million pounds weight, and it is thought that about seven million pounds weight were smuggled.

The price of teas sold by the East India Company from 1750 to 1783 averaged about four shillings and sixpence a pound, but the duties raised the average wholesale price to over seven shillings and sixpence a pound.[181] The approximate retail prices were as follows:

for black teas: Bohea, 5s. to 8s. per lb; Congou, 5s. to 16s. per lb; Pekoe and Souchong, 10s. to 18s. per lb, and for green teas: Singlo, 10s. to 12s. per lb; Hyson, 12s. to 18s. per lb.

It became necessary to avert a further decline in sales. In 1783, William Richardson published a second pamphlet[139] which dealt not with adulteration but with the whole problem of smuggling. In it he argues a case to beat smuggling by removing 'all the present Duties of Customs and Excise on Tea...'. His advice was heeded, and in 1784 Pitt introduced the Commutation Act by which the duty on tea was commuted to an *ad valorem* duty of 2½d to 6½d per lb., thus effectively reducing the tax from 119 per cent to 12½ per cent. To compensate for the expected loss of revenue, he increased the window tax[54] and introduced a brick tax. Within twelve months of the Act being passed the quantity of tea sold was nearly 15,000,000 pounds weight.[182] The increased consumption of tea may have helped to reduce the death rate, for 'both its rise and fall have been attributed in part to the growth and decline of the habit of drinking cheap gin instead of beer. After the middle years of the century tea became a formidable rival to alcohol with all classes.'[175,176]

Thus it was due largely to the smugglers' well organised enterprise and cut prices that the habit of tea drinking spread throughout the United Kingdom and into the poorest homes. From the potters' point of view this resulted in an increased demand for teawares.[55]

The year 1784 was also an auspicious one for the potters, for not only did the Commutation Act lead to a great increase in the demand for tea and thus teawares, but the duty on silver plate was also re-imposed. This duty could represent up to 25 per cent of the selling price of a piece. A six shilling teapot, for example, went up in price to about nine shillings. This increase must have encouraged people to consider buying a cream-ware teapot instead of a silver one, and the further

increase of duty on silver plate to one shilling per ounce in 1797 must have been a further impetus.[24] The decline at the same time in the importation of porcelain from China, both of full sets and replacements, created a real market for a reasonably priced porcelain. This need was met by bone china, formulated by the first Josiah Spode and marketed after his death by his son Josiah Spode II who introduced it in about 1799.

CHAPTER ONE: NOTES

I   See Appendix I.
II   At this time in Canton 3 Taels were equivalent to £1 sterling.
and the growth of population in the Potteries between 1740 and 1840.

III   *Kintledge* was the pig iron placed in ships' holds to act as ballast, and *dunnage* the loose wood or faggots laid above that to keep the cargo clear of the bilge water. Any cargo, such as porcelain, placed there for the same purpose — in this case as floorings for tea — was also classed as dunnage.[141]

IV   Table 1 (p. 164) compares imports and sales of tea, chinaware and tea tax and prices.
V   Table 2 (p. 165) compares the importation and consumption of tea, the importation of porcelain and the growth of population in the Potteries.
VI   The following Acts of Parliament are referred to in the text.
19 Geo III Cap 69: An Act for the more effectually preventing the pernicious Practices of Smuggling in this Kingdom.
24 Geo III Cap 38: 'The Commutation Act'. An Act for repealing the several Duties on Tea.
39 Geo III Cap 59: An Act for permitting certain Goods, imported from the East Indies, to be warehoused.

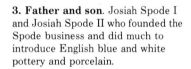

3. Father and son. Josiah Spode I and Josiah Spode II who founded the Spode business and did much to introduce English blue and white pottery and porcelain.

2 In imitation of the Chinese

IT IS NOT known in what sequence Spode introduced transfer-printed patterns. No record was kept and the only guide to the dates of introduction of some patterns is when enamelled colour was added; then the pattern was recorded in the famous Spode pattern books. It appears that two factors influenced Spode in his choice of printed patterns. First, his customers, when visiting his warehouse in London, might well have asked if Mr Spode could match this or that Chinese piece more quickly than they could obtain it by ordering it from Canton. Secondly, his newly engaged engraver, Thomas Lucas, would have brought with him, when he started work for Spode in 1783, some knowledge of the designs of his former employer, Thomas Turner at Caughley. Whatever the reason, the bulk of known surviving pieces of early blue transfer-printed wares of Spode are Chinese in style.

One consideration in dating a design is the style of the engraving. Nearly all the very early wares are engraved by line – usually coarsely, sometimes more finely. Later patterns show a limited use of stipple-punching, until eventually the engravers used both techniques to achieve the desired effect of tone and a sense of three dimensions. Another guide is the depth of blue colour. Generally, in early wares, the darker colours are the earliest, while some have a dull, greyish quality and others are in very deep cyanine blue. Only later were brighter or paler colours employed.

In view of this, the patterns will be dealt with in the following order: Willow Pattern and those directly related to it, Mandarin and Rock, the Landscape patterns, Buffalo pattern, Trophies type patterns, and finally the other patterns reproduced from Chinese originals. Where possible Spode's designs will be compared with those of other manufacturers, but it should be borne in mind that such comparisons are not conclusive evidence of design origins. It is known that potters bought white ware (undecorated glazed ware) from each other to help complete orders: they probably also bought biscuit ware (unglazed fired pottery). It also seems that lending of engravings sometimes took place, for reasons that are now unclear. Finally, and most importantly, sets of engravings were bought by successful potters from others selling up their businesses, and sometimes such engraved patterns were continued. More often the copper plates were knocked up – the backs were levelled by hammering the engraved face of the plate – and then planished smooth to take a new design. The Spode collection of engravings includes hundreds of such copper plates, both Spode patterns re-used and others bought in from outside. In instances where neither potter marked his name on all his wares, it is not possible to attribute finally the origin of a design.

The centre for manufacturing porcelain in China, at least for the European markets, was at Ching-tê-Chên, in Kiangsi Province. The potteries specialised in white bodied, resonant, translucent wares with transparent glazes of many colours, and decorations in cobalt underglaze colour and over-glaze enamel colours.[18] The wares for export were taken to the Yangtze Kiang river and carried by boat to Nanking, the port, 200 miles inland, from where the goods were shipped in junks to Canton about 1,200 miles to the South.[93] The other route was by way of Nanchang, where the wares were transferred to boats on the Kan River. At Nananfa, near the border of Kiangsi Province, they were carried overland through the Meiling Pass to Namyung on the North River which flowed past Canton.[109] This route was a mere six hundred miles.[135] (See fig. 1)

1. Map of China showing the locations of Ching-te Chen, Nanking, and Canton.

The more common wares were left undecorated or painted in cobalt blue under the glaze at Ching-t-Chên. Enamel colours could be added over the glaze in the china-painting workshops in Canton. Some of the blue and white wares sold to European merchants were decorated with landscapes, brocade-type borders and other motifs of purely Chinese origin. These designs continued in popularity into the nineteenth century and many were copied by English potters of whom Josiah Spode I was the most sympathetic to the Chinese style, and the most prolific. Only a fraction of the porcelains exported to Europe were made to special order, such as those carrying armorial bearings, monograms or reproductions of Western engravings.

However, the commissioning of such designs has given rise to the suggestion that Chinese landscape designs were invented in England – in Staffordshire specifically – and copied by the Chinese for export.[1] It is true that the Chinese did reproduce on porcelain copies after engravings supplied to them by foreign traders. Such designs cover a wide range of themes from religious subjects to sailing ships and kilted Scotsmen, but even when following Western designs the hand of the Chinese artist is evident: his style is significantly different. The Chinese painter, whether treating natural or contrived subjects, followed conventions derived from painters' manuals and ultimately from calligraphy. Willows, golden larch or prunus trees, temples, pavilions, fences and rockwork, all conform on Chinese porcelain to Chinese convention.[51] The British engravers adopted the designs but often in ignorance of the conventions. A Chinese picture is said to be a voiceless poem, in that every feature of, for example, a landscape, is held to correspond to human features and emotions. Thus water is regarded as the blood of the mountains, grass and trees the hair, and so on.[207] So British interpretations are often gentle misinterpretations, just as are Chinese versions of Western subjects.

In any event, other Chinese art forms readily supply the images that the ceramic artists translated into their work. Consider the roof of the pavilion, the style of the balustrade and the panelling in soapstone carvings of the Ming period, depicting ladies weighing a piece of jade or drinking tea. The roof especially recalls blue and white decorations, such as Buffalo pattern. (Fig. 2)

The fisherman's boat, carved in jade (Fig. 3), with his wife at the oar, is not so different from those depicted in Willow and Mandarin Patterns. The pavilions, walls and covered ways shown in the landscape illustrated (Fig. 4) are familiar even from a casual examination of the Temple Landscape or Two Temples patterns. The junk in Long Bridge Pattern may be fanciful to western eyes, but could be based on a Chinese painting such as that of a ship depicted on a Ming scroll. (Fig. 5)

And this surely was the process: the Staffordshire designer, whether matching an existing piece or not, followed the Chinese originals with as much skill and sympathy as he could muster. Just as there was no question of his work being

2. A soapstone carving of the seventeenth century. Notice the style of roof with decorated finial.

3. A fisherman with his net in the prow of a boat, his wife at the oar. A carving in jade.

5. A Ming ship depicted on a scroll. This is a junk of a design which might be compared with that in Long Bridge pattern.

mistaken for a Chinese original, so designs made in Chinese fashion in England but without a model are clearly recognisable as such.

One possible reason for the confusion as to originality is that handleless cups, similar to those used in Chinese tea ceremonies but of English manufacture, are among the earliest blue and white wares found. Briefly the difference between the Chinese and European methods of taking tea is that the Chinese infused the tealeaves in the tea bowl and the Europeans in the teapot. The Chinaman placed the leaves in the teacups and poured

4. Landscape with pavilions: two panels of a screen.

on boiling water from a spouted pot, probably a wine pot, which may be like a Cadogan teapot. A saucer was placed over the top to avoid loss of heat and water vapour. After infusion, the saucer was removed, placed on the tray and the clear liquid poured into it. The tea was drunk from the saucer: hence the term 'a dish of tea'.[147] The Chinese added neither sugar nor milk, preferring the pure and delicate taste of the tea. Milk, had they used it, would have damaged the surface of the furniture, because lactic acid destroys the fine lacquer finish of so much Chinese furniture. In the first hundred years or so after porcelain and tea reached England, the beverage was drunk from unhandled teacups, or tea bowls, and only later were requests sent for cups with handles. Because some Chinese services had tea bowls originally,

many English blue-printed replacements are also without handles.

As to the English ritual, in the eighteenth century it could be an extremely elegant, upper-class event at which the flavour of the tea, an expensive commodity, was only marred by gossip or other conversation! (Fig. 6) The tea service comprised: teacups, saucers (which would serve for teacups or coffee cups), deep round plates (for cake, biscuits, or bread and butter), a slop basin, a sugar bowl or covered sugar box, milk or cream jug, spoon tray (mostly with porcelain services, seldom with earthenware), teapot and teapot stand (to protect the furniture from the heat when teapots had flat bases). A combined tea and coffee service had only extra coffee cups: small tea plates were not introduced until after 1840.

6. A detail from 'The artist and his family at tea'. The cups and saucers are of Chinese porcelain. Attributed to Richard Collins, *c*. 1732. *Reproduced by courtesy of the Worshipful Company of Goldsmiths, London.*

The Chinese used cups without handles, while Europeans used cups with and without handles of various sizes for drinking their coffee, tea and chocolate.[148]

Particularly when such tea services were imported, owners would need replacements for breakages, or additions as their families enlarged: the same applies of course to dinner services. The decline in imports affected availability of such matchings, so that not only did a market opportunity present itself to the growing home pottery industry, but the work involved in producing matching sets gave potters the chance to familiarise themselves with Chinese originals.

Thomas Turner at Caughley was first to respond to this chance, and from the evidence of his Rag Book of engraved designs he reproduced five or six popular Chinese designs on porcelain. The next potter in line was Josiah Spode I who copied faithfully at least twenty-two Chinese originals (more than any other potter) and interpreted, sympathetically to the Oriental idiom, many more. The earliest of these productions were Buffalo, Two Figures, Rock and Mandarin: Pearl River House, Buddleia and Temple Landscape are also early.[II] The other patterns are datable after 1800, except for Willow, probably introduced in about 1795. Some patterns date from the significant changes of taste of the mid-1820s. But the dating of patterns produced in the closing years of the eighteenth and early years of the nineteenth centuries is almost impossible to achieve exactly.

It cannot therefore be asserted that hand painted patterns on creamware preceded those printed by transfer: but such precedence seems likely, as a form of blue painting was common earlier in the century.

Tin-glazed earthenware produced in such coastal towns as London, Bristol and Liverpool was decorated with blue painted designs. In North Staffordshire the earliest use of cobalt decoration was on salt-glazed stoneware. Probably inspired by the German stonewares then popular in Britain, a design was incised or scratched into the clay, and the lines were filled with a powdered cobalt compound such as zaffres. On firing the blue developed to yield an attractive form of decoration. Most of the pieces of this scratch blue seem to have been made during the third quarter of the eighteenth century.

Creamware manufacture, with two separate firings, provided a suitable surface for painting, and it is likely that blue painted creamware was made in considerable quantity in England until early in the nineteenth century. Most of the surviving examples are on a shell edge shape, where the edge of the ware was moulded to produce a continuous border of deep scratches tapering away from the edge, itself often scalloped. Few such wares are marked with a maker's name.[III]

Simeon Shaw, the historian of the Staffordshire Potteries, in introducing an account of Spode's contribution to the industry, published in 1829, writes:

'After Mr Josiah Spode left the employment of Mr Whieldon at Fenton, he was employed along with the late Mr Charles Harvey, in the manufactory of Mr Banks, on White Stone Ware, and for Cream Colour, Scratched and Blue Painted. But Messrs. Baddeley and Fletcher discontinuing making Porcelain, at Vale Lane, Shelton, Mr Spode commenced making the pottery most in demand – Cream Colour and Blue Painted, White Ware; and his productions were of tolerable excellence. His family remained resident in Stoke; and Messrs. Banks and Turner separating and Mr Banks relinquishing business in a short time afterwards. Mr S engaged the manufactory, (which subsequently he purchased) and there manufactured also Black printed, and Black Egyptian.'[158]

Shards excavated on the Spode factory show a characteristic type of shell edge which has a periodic overlap resulting in a small, buttonhole appearance[IV] (Fig. 7). Two of the shards have had the blue applied and hardened on by firing, but are unglazed, so proving that the blue was applied onto the biscuit ware.

7. Shard of Shell-edge ware excavated on the Spode factory. Creamware. The two small rim sections are unglazed, but the blue edge has been 'hardened-on'.

Three styles of decoration attributable to this part of Spode's career are known: a blue band at the edge, a blue edge stroked inwards along the moulding with sprays and festoons painted on the centre and rim (Fig. 8), and a similar edge with the House and Fence design (Fig. 9). The very fine dish strainer, or drainer (Fig. 10), is impressed with the large SPODE mark and incorporates a with the large SPODE mark and incorporates a border identical to the nankin[V] of the shell edge dish in figure 10, but with a wavy line added below. The dish is unmarked but shape, quality and feel of it suggest it could be of Spode's make. The plate in figure 7 is impressed SPODE, while the dessert service (Figs. 11 and 12) with gold decoration is impressed with the very large SPODE mark, and shows a strong resemblance to a Caughley piece.[VI]

The popularity of the House and Fence pattern may have given Spode a notion that a market existed for accurate copies of Chinese patterns rather than the chinoiserie pastiches similar to delftware then prevalent.[102] Certainly at this time he was also turning his attention to perfecting the printing process. Indeed the introduction of blue printing soon caused the end of blue painting, though, as Shaw relates, the painters of the Potteries district 'employed every artifice to prevent its success, but without avail'. There was one notable exception. 'When Blue Printing was introduced, the enamellers waited upon Mr Wedgwood to solicit his influence in preventing its establishment. We are informed that he religiously kept his promise. "I will give you my word, as a man, that I have not made, neither will I make, any Blue Printed Earthenware".'

CHAPTER TWO: NOTES

I One authority for this was W.B. Honey who wrote in *English Pottery & Porcelain* (1933) A & C Black. p.190, 'Two famous blue-printed patterns supposed to have been designed for Turner by the young Thomas Minton are the "Willow-Pattern" (both subject and legend are, I believe, purely European inventions) and the so-called "Broseley Blue dragon";....' and again, pp. 222-3, 'Exact copies of the late Chinese "export" blue-and-white were made in Spode's stone-china, and some of the heavy dishes in this style roughly glazed over the brownish body beneath are at times hard to distinguish from the actual Chinese, which had been copied from English models, perhaps even from the Spode wares themselves.' Note Spode's stone china dishes were made without any foot rim, and rough, but the body is the same all through.

II The names of some of the Spode patterns are not definitely known. Factory record books sometimes suggest names that are little known, indeed sometimes the same name is given to two different patterns. Leonard Whiter has

8. Plate 24.6cm. Pearlware. Shell-edge shape, blue painted underglaze in Cyanine blue 105. No foot. SPODE

suggested some names, derived from these records, which link onto the border designs. Where the centre designs are different this can be confusing, and in such cases alternative names are suggested here.

III George Miller of Parks Canada is engaged on a study of these blue scratch wares, in the hope of forming a guide to makers.

IV 'On the factory', though perhaps not perfect English, is traditional usage in Stoke on Trent, and is for that reason adopted here.

V Some export porcelains were known as Nanking , taking that name from the port from which they were shipped to Canton: there was no manufacture of porcelain at Nanking. It is confusing that this name was corrupted to *Nankeen* and that, later, collectors have given this name to various blue and white patterns. In the ships' manifests of the East India Company a clear distinction is made between Nankeen and chinaware. The cargo of the English ship *True Briton* despatched from Canton in 1754 consisted of:

Black Tea	1951	Piculs*
Green Tea	871	"
Raw Silk	162	Pieces
Woven Silk	706	"
Nankeen cloth	1200	"
Chinaware	102	Chests

* A picul is 133⅓ pounds weight or 100 catties
(Source: Morse Vol. V, p.19)

It is obvious that Nankeen is not porcelain: in fact it is a buff-coloured cotton cloth used especially for breeches, and first made at Nanking. There is further confusion because ceramic historians have applied the name Nanking to a particular class of porcelain decoration, but there is hardly any evidence to support their use of this terminology. The term *nankin* has been used in some Staffordshire pottery factories to refer to the inner border of a pattern which is applied below the shoulder of a plate and is usually about half an inch wide. The term nankin is here used when referring to an inner border of whatever design, despite the risk of confusing the name still further.

VI This piece is illustrated in Geoffrey Godden's *Caughley and Worcester Porcelains, 1775-1800,* as plate 52.

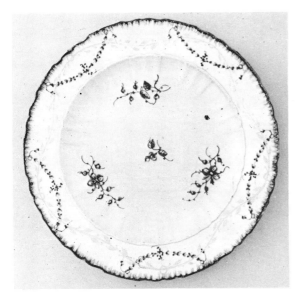

12. Dessert Plate *d.* 20.2cm. Pearlware (crazed and stained). Painted with sprigs, festoons and scratch edge in Cyanine 105, with linking festoons and edge hand gilded. SPODE

9. Oval meat dish Pearlware, painted
with House and Fence pattern.
Unmarked.

SPODE

10. Oval dish drainer 29.2 cm. *l.*
Pearlware. Painted in dark blue with an
elaborate chinoiserie subject in the
style of the House and Fence pattern.
*Photograph by courtesy of Harold
Holdway, Esq.*

SPODE

11. Dessert dish 24.1 cm. *l.* Pearlware
(crazed and stained). Painted with
sprigs, festoons and scratch edge in
Cyanine 1 0 5, with linking festoons and
edge hand gilded.

3   Cobalt Blue: its history as a ceramic colour

Spode put an inscription (Fig. 1) on some of his wares to commemorate the use of British cobalt in 1816. But the use of cobalt as a blue colouring material is considerably earlier. A necklace composed of blue glass beads coloured with cobalt, discovered in the north west of Iran, has been dated to about 2250 BC. Cobalt was used for colouring the hair dark blue on statuettes found in Egyptian tombs of the 5th Dynasty (2680-2530 BC).[5] Ceramic glazes containing cobalt dating back to 1200 BC are known from finds in Ethiopia, Mycenae and Tiryns, presumably imported thither from Egypt or Phoenicia.[114]

This BLUE-WARE is printed from the CALX of British COBALT, produced from Wheal Sparnon Mine in the County of Cornwall. August 1816.

1. Inscription on early nineteenth century Spode ware.

Cobalt was used by the potters of Persia and Syria for several centuries before the Chinese started to use it. Abu'l Qāsim's *Treatise on Ceramics,* known from two manuscripts, mentions cobalt in two chapters, the latter entry giving an account of the source of cobalt:[2]

'The sixth material is the stone lājvard, which the craftsmen call Sulaimāni. Its source is the village of Qamsar in the mountains around Kashan, and the people there claim that it was discovered by the prophet Sulaiman. It is like white silver shining in a sheath of hard black stone. From it comes lājvard colour, like that of lājvard-coloured glaze etc. Another type comes from Farangistān and is ash-coloured and soft. And there is a red kind found in the mine which is a deposit on the outside of the stones and is like the red shells of pistachios. This kind is very strong but is a fatal deadly poison.'[I]

A more exact geological description is offered by A.H. Schindler, Director of Mines in the area towards the end of the last century. He described thus the situation of Qamsar:

'The rocks are dolomites broken through by serpentines with an immense lode of iron ore, copper pyrites, sulphuret of nickel, cobalt bloom and earthy cobalt.'[II]

Pottery made in China during the T'ang Dynasty (AD 618-907) used cobalt on some pieces, the mineral most certainly being imported from Persia along the caravan route: it was therefore known as Mohammedan Blue.[17] During the Ming Dynasty 450 years later, native sources of cobalt were being worked, though the blues obtained at first were not so pure as from the imported material.[58] This is perhaps because the main ore mined was asbolite,[188] an impure mixture of manganese and other oxides containing variable quantities of cobalt oxide. Near Eastern sources produced arsenates such as cobaltite and danaite, a compound of cobalt and nickel which when refined yields a purer blue.[188,121]

The arrival of the first pieces of blue and white from China led to a search in Europe for sources for the blue colour. Silver-cobalt deposits at Schneeberg in Saxony were worked from the fifteenth century, and in 1520, a Frenchman, Pierre Wiedenhammer,[6] made a blue colour from ores from Erzgebirge in Saxony, which he sold in Venice under the name of 'saffre' (or 'zaffre') as a colourant for glass beads. The unusual name 'zaffres' may be a corruption of 'sapphire'.

The mines of the Erzgebirge region are described by Agricola in his *Bermannus: De re Metallica Dialogus,* published in 1530.[6] He uses the term Kobelt to describe an ore found in the silver workings: it injured the miners' hands and feet in the wet and affected their lungs and eyes. Kobelt was therefore probably an arsenical cobalt. In the Harz Mountains, certain ores from copper mines when roasted gave off dangerous fumes, and were therefore referred to as Kobold – mischievous spirits. The origin of the elemental name cobalt is therefore this malicious sprite who troubled miners so.

Smalts are the double silicate of cobalt and potassium, and are a workable form of the element. The process for producing smalts was devised by Christian Schurmer of Neudeck in Bohemia, in about 1540.[III] Thus by the late sixteenth century Saxony had become an important area for production of cobalt, and Prince Augustus in 1575 granted a sole concession to Harrer and Jenitz, to prepare colour from the ores mined in Schneeberg. The royal concessionaires were ruined by smuggling and other competition, despite the protection of royal decrees, and in 1609 control passed into the Prince's own hands. His decree of 1603 is interesting in that it refers to the considerable quantity of oxide bought by Dutch merchants for re-sale in Holland, England and Spain – 'over four thousand hundred weight'.[21]

A large proportion of such cobalt imported into England was in the form of smalts, used in the linen trade to whiten cloth, but some must have been for decorating tin-glazed ware. The volume of imports rose over the years, reaching such a level that the Society for the Encouragement of the Arts (later the Royal Society of Arts) decided to try and stimulate home production. Figures given in the Society's *Transactions* show that in 1754 imports totalled 286,739 pounds weight, as opposed to 179,564 pounds weight in 1748.[171] The Society therefore offered a premium or prize of £30 for producing specimens of cobalt discovered in the United Kingdom, properly authenticated both as to origin and availability in quantity.[170] This premium was won in May 1775 by Francis Beauchamp. He offered samples from Pengreep, a mine near Truro in Cornwall, which were tested for the Society by Nicholas Crisp. A month earlier

the Society had offered a further premium of £30: 'for making the most and best Zaffer & Smalt from English Cobalt not less than 5lb weight of Zaffer and 15lb weight of Smalt: to be produced on or before the second Wednesday in January 1756 with satisfactory certificates'.[169] This first premium does not, however, seem to have been awarded, and the offer was repeated in December 1756, when only one pound of zaffre was sought. The premium carries this interesting preamble: 'Zaffer being used in the painting of China and Earthern Ware, and smalt in the composition of powder blue, both which articles are constantly imported from abroad to the amount of about 300,000lb weight annually, it is therefore proposed ....' It is clear that great difficulty was incurred in producing a suitable zaffre or smalt from British cobalt: the premium was finally awarded to Nicholas Crisp in 1764.[188] It seems that the first furnace in the Potteries for extracting blue was set up in about 1772 by Roger Kinnaston, who had been instructed in the art by the chemist and painter William Cookworthy.[154] The market for cobalt was considerable, and the product expensive: a note in the Wedgwood archives concerns, for example, the price of oxides imported from Sweden.[IV] However, an unpublished account of a visit by Mr Carter Smith to a Norwegian cobalt mine in 1838 may be of interest.

17 August – 'In the evening we started for Fossum, to visit the Works for refining Cobalt (i.e. the Foulfiend-Kobald.) These works were likewise purchased by a Company of Germans, just 20 years ago, for 60 m. Dollars. Having been long unproductive in the hands of the Danish Government, they now produce a large income, and are the largest and best works for quality in the world. The Cobalt is found in the neighbouring mountains in the granular state, in union with quartz, granite etc. – is first provided in the mass in Mills – is subsequently washed, sifted and cleansed until all the earthy, and principally siliceous parts are got rid of. It is then roasted for 12 hours to throw off the arsenic, sulphur, etc. combined with it – and being purified and oxydized with a flux of white quartz, is in the state called Zaffres – which is used by our manufacturers of Blue China. If required for Smalts, the ore is combined with white quartz and potass, and being fused for 12 hours is reduced to an intense Blue Glass, almost black. This is subsequently ground, washed and sifted until a very fine powder is obtained. This then is dried in ovens and packed in casks of 3½ cwt. The principal consumption of both Smalts and Zaffres is in England.

These works employ about 100 men in the Fabrication and 900 in mining. Their establishment includes a Chemist, Surveyor of Mines, Physician and a Commercial Department of Clerks. The Chemist has £300 to £400 per year, varying according to produce of the works – with a complete House &

Establishment provided for him – wood – garden etc. The workmen obtain abt. 1 marc, or 10^d per day – and have constant employ throughout the year – the aged, sick and married with their wives and children are maintained by the Proprietors, and by a deduction of 1 schilling in every 120 of their wages – which are paid partly in food and clothing and the remainder in cash.

The Produce of these works is certainly worth 30 m £ per annum. They cost about 12 m £, – the outlay in Buildings cannot have been less than 100 m.£, and the annual Expenses may be ab^t 15 m £ per ann. – so that about 15 m £ remains to pay Interest on Outlay 5 m, & Profit 10 m, which is not more than sufficient.

Opposite to the works is a Timber-shoot, down the side of a Hill, whence logs are precipitated into the Dram River from the S: – & through the works passes a Timber conduit by which Deal & Logs enter it from the N. Both these are sources of Profit to the Works. Their consumption of wood is very large – it is all cut on the Estate attached to them, and may be estimated at... in fathoms and costs 2 marcs or 21d. per fathom of 6 x 6 x 2 = 72 cub. feet.

While here a fine salmon was brought from the neighbourhood of Hogsund, which weighed 25lbs. and for which 12 marcs or 10/- Engl. was demanded, ab.^{t} 5d. p lb. This was thought dear, and 8 marcs were offered and refused.[104] *(The quantity of timber is not given in the original.)*

Even by 1835 the price, as noted in the collection of Spode manuscripts for June 3rd, could still be twenty shillings a pound.[111]

British cobalt came from a number of mines in Cornwall, notably Wheal Sparnon (Fig. 2). Usually it was a by-product of copper or tin mining, and only Wheal Sparnon seems to have seriously exploited the deposits, establishing their own refining plant in 1816. Ore from this mine could be worth at best £200 a ton, and its quality was endorsed by a certificate dated April 1817 signed by Josiah Wedgwood II and other Staffordshire potters.[188] Other mines that produced cobalt in any quantity were Truro Mine near St Columb, and St Austell Consols Mine, St Stephen. Other mines such as Botallack, St Just; Wheal Herland; Wherry Mine, Penzance or Dolcoath Mine, Camborne, produced less than a ton each.[V] But whatever the production of English mines, a great deal of cobalt, particularly of the best quality, continued to be imported from Saxony in the eighteenth and Scandinavia in the nineteenth century. A brief discussion of the chemical properties and structure of cobalt may explain somewhat the problems and complexities faced by the potter.

Cobalt 'colour' in fact results from cobalt oxide. The principal compounds found as ores are cobaltite ($CoAsS$), and smaltite ($CoAs_2$). The

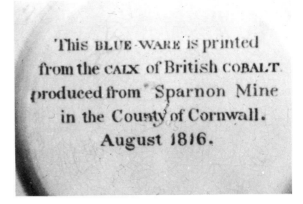

2. Alternative inscription correcting the name of the mine.

inclusion of arsenic (As) and Sulphur (S) in these ores being, to say the least, unfortunate, the earliest form of oxide was produced by simply roasting the ores in sand to volatize the sulphur and arsenic. The resulting product was known as zaffres. If the zaffre was fused with potassium carbonate, it became a potash silica glass coloured by cobalt: this was known as smalts.[30] Several oxides of cobalt are used in pottery production, but only the monoxide, cobaltous oxide (CoO), is stable over 800 °C, and can therefore be used for underglaze transfer prints. The most important compounds of cobaltous oxide used as colourants are the silicate and the aluminate. The former is usually known as mazarine, royal, or cobalt blue, the latter as matt blue: chemists sometimes use the term Thénard's blue.[VI] Various metallic oxides can be added to these compounds to vary the tone and hue of the resulting blues.

An underglaze colour must have two components, the colour stain (which must be stable and brilliant when glazed and fired) and the flux to fasten the colour to the biscuit body. The glaze has an important effect on brilliance and unfortunately a glaze that gives particularly high brilliancy may often have a high solvent action, which impairs equally the fineness of the pattern. So it is very unusual to find underglaze patterns in cobalt silicate blues especially in which the lines and dots of the pattern are not to some degree blurred, for the intensity of the cobalt silicate reveals the slightest diffusion of colour into the glaze. This 'running' of underglaze blue was deliberately exploited in the nineteenth century with the production of *flow blue*, in which a suffused blue haze surrounds the printed image, if it does not cover the whole piece. This effect was achieved by putting flow powder – a mixture of salt (sodium chloride), white lead and calcium carbonate – into the saggars during firing.

The development of blue designs was thus a matter both of technology and taste. The early designs were very dark, both in imitation of Chinese originals and because the potters' control over chemistry was not well developed. Later both engraving techniques and colour compounds permitted paler blues, which were increasingly to English taste in the early nineteenth century – until the introduction of flow blue. And export wares, particularly for the southern states of the USA, were often printed dark, as strong sunlight 'washed out' pale colours. Therefore, the lightness or darkness of blue in a piece cannot be regarded as the only method of dating it.

The technique of the potter was a developing one, not only in the form and decoration of wares, but also in the chemical technology of potting. This diversity and development may be seen in the Appendix, which lists some of the formulae and recipes used in the Spode factory over the years, taken from the Recipe Book still kept in the Director's safe in the boardroom at Spode.[VII]

CHAPTER THREE: NOTES

I   The translation is by J.W. Allan,[3] who noted in his commentary that sang-i lajvard is the Persian for lapis lazuli. Cobalt ore could have the same name as it was used with shukat-i sang (quartz) and shakar (soda) to make gemstones in imitation of lapis lazuli.

II   The full description of the production and use of cobalt from these mines given by Schindler will be found in the appendix to this chapter on p. 166.

III Bruchmueller's account of the production of smalts is given in the appendix. (b)

IV   A letter to Josiah Wedgwood II from John Leslie, enclosing examples of Swedish cobalt, is given in the appendix.

V   I am particularly grateful to Richard Barstow of Geevor Mine, Pendeen, for the information on mines producing cobalt. He also very kindly drew my attention to A.K. Hamilton-Jenkins: *Mines and Miners of Cornwall.*

VI   Despite some assertions to the contrary,[101] Thénard's blue is not an artificial ultramarine, which is today manufactured from china clay, sulphur and sodium carbonate together with a little pitch, coal or oil.[145] Artificial ultramarine contains no cobalt, and, as tests at the Spode laboratory in 1978 showed, is quite useless as a high temperature ceramic colourant. The main use of artificial ultramarine is as a pigment for plastics and paints. The term ultramarine blue describes a particular hue, which can of course be obtained on ceramics with a cobalt-based dye.

VII For these entries see page 168.

4 The Manufacturing Process

THE QUALITY of any printed reproduction depends on the original from which it is taken. In ceramic printing, it is the standard of engraving quality which in the first place decides the appearance of the transferred print. The process of origination is as follows. The designer prepares a drawing on paper, usually for a ten-inch dinner plate – the central item of a tableware service. From this design an engraving is made for a sample plate and carefully checked. Only then are drawings for the other items in the service prepared, by sketching the outline only on the actual piece, and taking a tracing once the correct proportions have been obtained. One of the pottery designer's chief problems has always been to think in terms of several different three-dimensional articles which can live together in any combination.

The tracings of the designs taken from actual items will make unusual shapes when transferred to paper, and the curves and contours of the piece can only be successfully decorated if the 'fittings' of the pattern are carefully checked. Up to about 1810, few pieces were fully engraved, that is, with border and centre specially drawn item by item. Often only plates, cups and saucers received such attention, because the quantities manufactured and sold justified the cost. For other items such as dishes, teapots or cream jugs, a selection of centre patterns in different sizes, and strips of borders in differing widths, called straight lengths, would be prepared and adapted to fit in each case, be it eggcup or meat dish.

Before the coming of photography, designs were traced by the engraver onto oiled tissue paper. Using a carbon paper (prepared by rubbing a black-lead pencil all over one side of a tissue paper) he obtained an outline of the design on the copper plate which had its surface 'sized', or smeared with a mixture of turps and resin. This faint pencil image was made more permanent by going over the pencil lines with a sharp, hard steel point.

Next, these lines were engraved using a 'graver' or 'burin', a very hard steel tool of lozenge section, which is pushed through the copper to cut out a V-section line.[26] Very early prints on ceramics suggest that the copper plates were engraved only by the burin, but another technique was developed which was especially used for shading and for providing a tone over a large area, This is called 'stipple-punching' and is achieved with a sharp pointed steel punch which is struck with a small hammer. This also makes a V-shaped hole. (Fig. 1)

It is of course possible to etch designs onto the copper plate with acid, but the acid eats a hole which has parallel sides and a flat base, like ⊔. When the colour is applied it is difficult to push it into the sharp corners and, even more importantly, the colour is not pulled out of them when the tissue paper is removed. A rough-edged line or dot results which yields a messy appearance. Etched coppers, therefore, are seldom used except for a subject to be reproduced very faintly, when the resulting trough is so shallow as not to present a problem. At least two coppers for Chinese landscapes in the Spode collection show that some parts have been etched, which yields a rough-edged line, while other parts have been engraved.

The process of engraving has altered little since about 1800 by which time the present techniques were known and practised. (Figs.2 and 3) Today, the engraver will cut lines and punch dots over the whole design before scraping off the 'burr' created at the edges of the engraving. Then, those

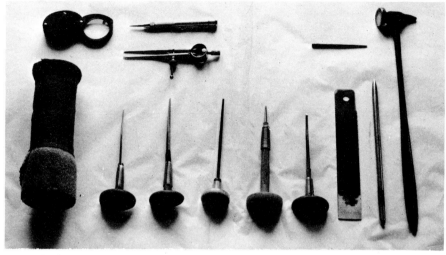

1. A burin and other engraver's tools.

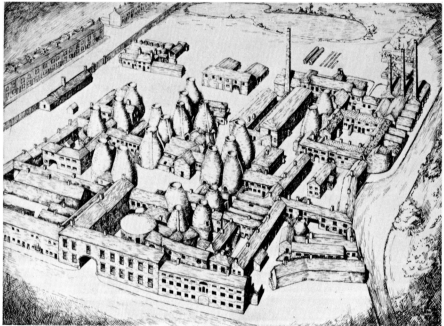

2. Spode's factory in Stoke-upon-Trent, 1820-35. The main road from Uttoxeter to Burslem passes by the front entrance (in foreground). The packing house was close by and the large round house (demolished about 1928) may have been a threshing floor so that Spode could have a convenient supply of straw for packing his wares. *Drawing by Harold Holdway from earthenware model in Spode Museum.*

areas of shading or outlines which require to be deepened to yield a darker colour will be 're-entered': that is, the line or dot will be deepened by cutting a deeper line, or giving the punch another tap with the hammer. A second scraping will follow to yield an engraving from which a trial print may be taken: the engraver can see from this if any further work is needed.

When the engraving has been passed, trial prints pulled and transferred to a piece of ware to ensure that the final effect is correct when the colour has been fired. If so, the copper is plated, first with nickel, later with steel, to render the surface less liable to scratching and increase its useful life.[1]

The process of getting the print onto the ware is achieved in two separate stages: the print is made from the engraved copper plate first, and this is then passed to the transferring team for application to the item. This technique has hardly changed since the nineteenth century, although the process here described is modern. (Fig. 4)

PRINTING SHOP.

3. Printer's Square, *c.* 1890. The printing team worked in this area, which was close to the dipping house and glost ovens.

4. A printing shop in the 1890s with coal-fired stoves.

The equipment needed consists of a hot plate A (see fig. 5), on the end of which rests a circular 'backstone' B. This iron plate should reach a warmth sufficient to keep the colour in a workable condition. A flat steel table C is at right angles to these. A wooden table, D, supports the sloping desk, E, on which the tissue paper will be wetted with soap 'size'. The roller press, F, stands on the floor. The 'colour' – a mixture of metallic and inorganic compounds with oil – is placed on the backstone, where it is stirred about until ready for use. The copper plate is put onto the hot plate to heat up. Meanwhile the printer cuts several sheets of tissue paper to the dimensions he needs, and, placing each one on the sloping desk, he

brushes over it a solution of soft soap and water from a bowl to his right. The purpose of the 'size', as this solution is called, is to prevent the tissue paper being singed on the hot copper, to enable it to be as flexible as possible for application, and to make it easier to remove in water after the printed pattern has been secured to the piece of ware (this only applies in the case of underglaze transferring onto the biscuit ware). The size also renders the paper impervious to oil.

Colour is placed on the copper plate and rubbed well into the engraving with a wooden 'dabber'. The surplus colour is scraped off with a metal blade, though formerly wooden scrapers, which quickly wore out, were used. This leaves a thin film of colour. The copper is carried over to the steel table where the film of colour is removed by deftly padding it sideways with a boss, a large pad faced with corduroy fabric.

The copper is placed on the iron plank of the press where a sheet of newly re-sized tissue paper is carefully placed over it. The lever of the press is pulled by the printer towards him, which turns the upper roller so that the plank passes between both rollers. The upper roller is covered with layers of felt which, pressing onto the tissue paper, forces it into contact with the colour in every engraved line and dot.

On reversing this procedure the copper plate is returned to the hot plate to soften the colour

5. Floor plan of a flat printing press.

6. (*left*) **Cutting out transfers** The young girl often stood up so that the tissue paper did not crease by coming into contact with the workbench.

7. (*right*) **The transferring area** The print is being rubbed down.

slightly as the printer eases the tissue from its surface.

The printed image is tacky, so this is kept facing upwards until the act of placing it in position. First the surplus paper is cut away with scissors or with a glass-cutting wheel, using a revolving disc as a cutting table: the girl who performs this task is called the 'cutter'.(Fig. 6)

The transferrer places the different sections of the print in position on the piece of ware (Fig. 7). Joins are carefully matched and prints round handles, spouts and knobs skilfully fitted. She will gently rub the back of the paper with a small piece of felt to allow the colour to hold in position. The print is now rubbed down vigorously with a stiff-bristled brush to ensure the colour is thoroughly transferred to the porous biscuit earthenware.[11]

The paper cannot be left on during firing because some colour remains on it and this when fired would disfigure the pattern. After the paper has been washed off in cold water, every item is inspected to ensure that the print has been correctly transferred.

The colour must now be fixed to the ware. This is achieved by firing at between 680 and 750°C – just about red heat – to enable the fluxes in the colour mixture to combine with the surface of the biscuit ware, and to drive off the oils.

Glaze is applied by several methods today, but in the eighteenth and nineteenth centuries it was usually dipped by hand into a mixture of glass-forming ingredients, ground finely and suspended in water (Fig. 8). After firing in the 'glost' oven, the ware emerges with a brilliant glaze covering the coloured print.

The methods of placing ware in the 'glost' oven varied from factory to factory and were partly determined by the quality required and the cost of achieving this. (Fig. 9)

Saggars were used to contain the ware. These not only protected it from the open flames and fumes, but enabled an oven to be packed safely. The placing of ware into the saggars was done at a 'placing bench' in front of which were 'stillages' – vertical posts with projecting arms – on which the placer would rest boards carrying the unfired ware. (Fig. 10)

Best bone china flatware, such as plates and saucers, have always rested with their feet in some form of crank, carrying small triangular-

8. (*left*) **Dipping** The dipper is about to immerse the dish into the fluid glaze in the tub.

9. (*right*) **Glost placing** in the 1890s.

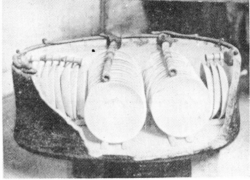

10. Saggars placed with cups and saucers.

section strips on which the piece stands, The foot of a bone china item as found on plates and saucers is for the express purpose of supporting it in the glost oven and decorating kiln. If a piece without a foot had to be fired three or four times, a very unsightly assortment of pin marks would be found on the back which would detract from its value and appearance.

Every other item of bone china also had a foot except meat dishes or platters, and teapot stands made in the very early days; these would be supported in the oven on stilts or spurs.

Best quality earthenware plates were placed on edge, or 'reared', so that only one pin mark occurred on the back of the rim, and two small areas of rim with little or no glaze on them. This method of 'rearing' gave blue prints the chance to 'run' down if the glaze was too thick or the oven too hot, an effect often seen in the foot rims of pearlware saucers, as the glaze carried some of the blue down the article as it ran.

Medium quality earthenware made by reputable manufacturers was 'dottled'. Between upper and lower plates were three pillars into which were inserted ceramic pins which supported the plates beneath their rims. These left three pin marks on the back, but no mark on the face. Early blue and white earthenware was not dottled, as thimbles were used to form the supporting pillars.

The lowest grades of ware, when the manufacturer seemed to be unconcerned with leaving marks on the face of the pieces, were placed face downwards and supported on 'spurs'. These 'spurs' had a single point on one side and three or four on the other. Usually three spurs were used to support a plate or platter by arranging them so that the plate would rest its rim on them. Probably a previously fired spoiled plate was placed on the bottom first. This method results in three sets of spur marks on the back of the plate (usually beneath the rim) and three single marks on the face of the piece.

Bowls were fired on their feet. Sometimes another piece was placed inside to save space, but even if a stilt was used to support the smaller item, ugly marks often resulted.

Large bowls, as used for toilet services, were separated by using 'dumps'.

Cups, being of low height, could be placed on their feet or on shelves or bats inside saggars and supported on conical props.

On the bottom of every saggar there was a layer of crushed flint grit, called bitstone, to provide an unglazed surface for resting ware of all sorts, but mainly hollow ware.

The marks left by some of these different systems of support have been detailed where they might provide a clue to identifying ware. In some cases it has been possible to identify individual factories that did not use any other form of mark, by their characteristic placing of supports.

The foregoing description is of the developed form of transfer printing, using tissue paper. However, there is increasing evidence that the earliest method of printing was by glue bat. In a paper to the English Ceramic Circle, delivered in October 1977, Colin Wyman quoted a description of bat-printing published by James Poulton in the *Liverpool Student* for 1799, under the title: *Of Transferring copperplate impressions to earthenware.*[80] (The text explains that in this account 'paper' refers to a glue bat.)

'1. *Of the preparation of the transferring paper:*
Take one pound of the best glue, soak it for six or eight hours in clean water, wipe its surface clean, put it into a glazed earthenware vessel and add to it half a pound of Barbadoes Tar. Let the vessel be put into boiling water and the ingredients stirred till they are well incorporated.
Next pour this mixture of glue and tar into a broad shallow dish to form a cake of about a quarter of an inch thick, and when cool it is fit for use.

2. *Of the oil for filling the engraved plate:*
Take one pint of linseed oil to which add a spoonful of pulverised umber. Let them boil for thirty or forty minutes and when cold the clear oil may be kept to be used with a little oil of turpentine. If the plate does not clean easily a few drops of Barbadoes Tar must be added to the oil which will cause it to work with ease.

3. *Of the press:*
The press is a piece of wood 12 or 14 inches long 9 inches broad and 7 or 8 inches high. The upper part must be rounded evenly and covered with three or four folds of flannel and over them must be neatly fixed a covering of smooth leather.

4. *Of the boss:*
The boss is made of a bag of soft smooth leather filled as much as possible with corded wool or bran. It is generally about 16 inches long and 12 broad.

5. *Of filling the plate and printing*
Take a bit of cotton, roll it into a ball, dip it in the prepared oil and rub the plate all over with the oil. Clean the plate with hand as in common copper plate printing. The transferring paper being cut to the proper size and laid upon the press, the plate must then be gently pressed upon it beginning at the nearer end and proceeding gradually to the other. The plate now being taken up the transfer paper will adhere to it which must be carefully separated from it, beginning at one end corner. The transfer paper is then placed upon the boss and the vessel to be printed pressed gently upon the printed side of the paper, beginning at one end and proceeding to the other. The paper being carefully separated from the vessel, the proper colour ground fine must be dusted on the printed part of the vessel with a piece of cotton wool, which will adhere to the oil left upon the vessel by the transferring paper. Any loose particles of dust must be wiped off with a handkerchief, and when the work is dry and properly cleaned, the vessel is fired, and the work completed.'

A further description of the process was given to Alison Griffin in 1978. This was probably the last use of bat-printing on ceramics.

Frank Boothby, master engraver at Spode Limited, described a man called Bruce who worked with Mr Boothby Senior. Bruce was the last of his family to be employed as bat printers at Spode and with his retirement in about 1887 Spode saw the end of bat printing. Bruce worked for W.T. Copeland & Sons when Mr Boothby Senior was an apprentice gilder. Because gilding is the final decorative process Mr Boothby Senior had frequent contact with Bruce in order to explain to him the areas on ware needing to be printed. Bruce's workshop was a very black, dirty and dark room. It was a long room with a bench covering the length of one side. On this bench there were many glost, twenty-inch, flat bottomed earthenware dishes. In the end corner there was a fire on which was a large cauldron.

The cycle of his work began at night when he would collect all the bats used that day and put them into the cauldron, where there was undoubtedly unused glue. He would boil all the bats up and then, when the glue was ready he would pour it into dishes in a line on the bench. He would then go home.

The following morning he would cut these bats to suit the coppers he was required to print from that day; they would be left on the dishes until required. He would be wearing an old printer's apron with a protective leather patch tied to his thigh. Before he commenced printing he would fix the smaller copper plates such as engraved crest outlines, onto a bat of wood with black tar. The plates thus prepared he would sit on his three-legged stool and start printing. Firstly he would saturate a cloth pad in linseed oil and using this rub his engraving, thus leaving a film of oil on the plate. Then he would rest his copper on his thigh and boss off all the excess oil, either with a soft boss or more often with the ball of his palm, first coating his hand with whiting to aid him. He would then place the bat on to a pad (probably made from leather and filled with bran, sawdust or corded wool) and roll it onto the copper, still on his knee. His next step was to make 'V' shaped nicks on the edges of the bat to ensure its fit and registration. He would then press the bat into place on the ware either by hand or his pad. No press was used, in contrast to the paper method. The glue bat was peeled off leaving an impression in oil on the ware which was dusted with colour using a piece of cotton wool. The excess colour was similarly removed to leave a printed design on the ware ready for firing and gilding. Bruce would continue printing all day in this manner until it was time to collect up his bats for re-boiling. Undoubtedly he would have cleansed his bats throughout the day with turpentine.(Fig. 11)

Bat printing was originally an aid to painting pottery. Simeon Shaw mentions how Wedgwood

sent his creamware to Sadler and Green in Liverpool to be printed, at least as early as 1767 to Shaw's certain knowledge (he had in fact been doing so since 1763).[III] Shaw[155] continues, 'The great demand for Blue Painted and Enamelled Pottery, caused an attempt to facilitate the process by forming the outline on the ware, from a Glue Bat, similarly to Black Printing, which could be readily filled in by the painter. This was first practised by William Davis, for Mr W Adams, Cobridge;...The method of printing with glue bats was also practised by Harry Baker, for Mr Baddeley of Shelton; about 1777, and very little progress was made in the practise for some time.' Shaw writes, 'But, the first black Printer in the district, is said to have been Harry Baker, of Hanley, prior to Sadler and Green practising it;...'[151]

Whether or not Baker was printing before Sadler is not known, for John Sadler swore an affidavit on 2 August 1756 that on 29 July 1756 with the assistance of Guy Green alone he had printed more tin-glazed tiles in six hours than could be painted by 'one hundred skilled pot painters in the like space of time'.

There is other evidence to support Shaw's thesis that Baker was printing in Hanley in the 1770s.[IV]

On 13 October 1781 Baker took out a Patent, No.1296, which included the preparation of oils and references to four processes of printing, two hot and two cold.[V]

The most important aspect of Baker's development of the process was the use of a paper treated with gum arabic (which was impervious to oil). Simeon Shaw was well aware of the value this had for the process:[156]

'The next stage in its improvement was employing paper and transferring it to the Pottery; but in this the printer proceeded very differently from the present method. The paper was different in texture and quality and was applied in a dry state. The Plates were so extremely strong that no delicate shades were preserved. The specimens have scarcely anything deserving the name of *a fine part*. And unless the printer was very expert in removing the paper from off the plate the instant it came from between the rollers, the greatest difficulty resulted; and while much loss in paper and colour occurred to the master, the workman both lost his labour for that impression, and had additional trouble to clean the plate prior to taking off another.'

One can speculate as to other reasons why a suitable paper was necessary before transfer printing could be fully developed. One is that

11. A simulation of Bat printing.

The oil is rubbed onto the engraved area using a piece of soft cloth. The oil used was a mixture of linseed oil and oil of turpentine or barbadoes.

The surplus oil is removed by wiping the copper plate with the hand.

The bat is rolled on to the copper plate using pad filled with sawdust or a similar substance.

The bat is peeled from the engraving very carefully to avoid blurring the printed pattern.

The bat, with the design printed on, is then rolled gently on the ware.

It is then removed equally carefully to reveal the design printed in oil on the ware.

Powdered colour is applied to the ware with a piece of cotton wool in this case, though reference has been made to colour being pounced on through a muslin bag.

The resulting print is now ready to be fired in an enamel kiln.

All the excess colour is removed from the ware using cotton wool.

tissue paper, especially when treated with liquid, becomes transparent, thus enabling the printer or transferrer to fit the pattern accurately. There is no record of the trial and error necessary to achieve such a paper, but it was not until 1797, when William Adams built paper mills on land at Cheddleton called Butcher's Meadow that a supply was available locally.[32] These mills were later let to Henry Fourdinier who made great improvements in the process.

A treated paper (and later a paper treated with soap size) could also be used with a hot printing process. When in 1783 the use of oils to bind the colour to the biscuit ware was perfected,[157] it became possible to print blue colour under the glaze, on earthenware as well as on china. Thus by 1815 the process of pottery manufacture had evolved to much like its modern state, and the best description is the one published in that year in *Ree's Manufacturing Industry*.[137] The difference between that account and the contemporary process are much less remarkable than the similarities.

The transfer from glue bat to paper transfer printing was of course a gradual one, but it represented a real change in attitude also. Bat printing was a method used mainly for on-glaze printing of china, an expensive commodity. Transfer printing allowed under-glaze printing on earthenware, being produced for a much wider market. The transfer printing team, though more numerous, worked faster, with the aid of a mechanical press, using plated coppers engraved at first more coarsely, that needed plating for their protection.[VI] The bat printer worked alone, applying the cold ink to bat and ware by hand. It was a slow process, requiring considerable skill. In short, bat printing was a craft process, while transfer printing was an industrial one.

Elsewhere in England transfer printing seems to have been practised earlier. Excavations on the Warmstry House site of Dr Wall's factory, discussed by Henry Sandon, provided underglaze printed pieces in strata datable to about 1760, and it seems that John Brooks, originally a Dubliner, was engraving in Birmingham as early as 1751.[VII] It took about twenty-five years, therefore, from the introduction of the method on porcelain to achieve a satisfactory result on biscuit earthenware.

CHAPTER FOUR: NOTES

I   In 1976 the nickel/steel plating process was replaced with chromium plating which rendered the surfaces even more proof against scratching.

II   In the case of prints applied on a glost surface, the rubbing process is omitted. When the colour of the transferred print is too pale, powdered colour may be rubbed into it after the paper has been removed: this is called 'pull and dust'. Blue prints are normally dark enough but the cobalt only develops its brilliant blue tones at the temperature of the glost fire, i.e. 1040 to 1080°C, so the ware is fired again at this heat. The colour is now said to be 'in-glaze'.

III   I am most grateful to Colin Wyman for drawing my attention to an entry in Sadler's accounts with Wedgwood which mentions a 'Salad Bowl Blue and White'. This is dated 21st May 1763 and thus gives an earlier date than any previous evidence.

IV   An earlier account of bat printing is quoted by Robert Charleston[28] from an extract of Lady Shelburne's diary written for 16th May 1766 when she visited Mr Taylor's enamel works in Birmingham.

V   The description of one of the two hot processes for printing on glass reads as follows:

'Take a sheet of thin paper and having dissolved some gum arabic in water, spread it with a pencil on one side of the paper; let it dry; then take one part of Number Two (balsam of amber) and one part of Number Three (Venice Turpentine) for ink; put the copper plate on a charcoal fire or stove to warm, and into this ink put such a colour as you please to print with, and rub it into the plate....put the plate with gummed paper on it through a rolling press, take it off the plate and put it on the glass; rub it with flannel to fix it to the glass, then soak in water, and the whole impression will quit the paper and be left on the glass.'

VI   Coppers for bat engraving were not scraped after use, and so remain in very good condition even today, and because they were not heated, and could be more finely engraved, were thinner than the plates used in transfer work. One supplier of such plates was the firm of Whittow & Harris,[80] whose trade card shows one man hammering out a copper plate and another planishing one.[88]

VII   John Mallet has drawn my attention to an article by Roberto Bondi in *Faenza* (No. 5, 1971) which explains that many pieces of porcelain made by the Doccia factory during its first twenty years from 1737 have been transfer printed under the glaze with cobalt blue decoration. Although it seems that the technique was only employed for a short time, and not attempted on glaze, Doccia can, on this evidence, claim priority over England in the use of transfer printing.

PRINTING BY TRANSFER: THE MODERN PROCESS

1 Spreading the colour over the engraving which rests on the hot stove. The wooden tool is called a 'dabber'.

4 'Sizeing' the tissue paper. This size is a solution of soft soap and water which is kept in the bowl (*in foreground*).

2 Scraping off the surplus colour which is returned to the 'backstone' (*top left*).

5 Placing the tissue onto the copper engraving which has been placed on the 'plank' of the printing 'press'.

3 'Bossing' the engraving to remove the thin film of colour left by the scraper.

6 Operating the lever which causes the plank with the engraving to pass between the rollers. The upper roller is covered with felt to help force the paper into contact with every line and dot of colour.

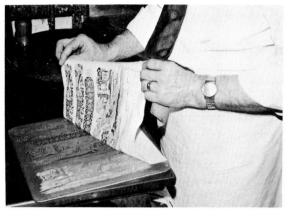

7 Pulling the print away from the engraving. This is done with the copper resting on the hot stove so that the colour is softened and does not cause the paper to stick to the surface.

TRANSFERRING

9 The transferrer places the prints into position and lightly rubs them down so that the tackiness of the colour holds them in their proper positions.

8 The parts of the print required to decorate the object are cut out of tissue paper by the 'cutter', who is the junior member of the transferring team of three. Here she uses a glass-cutting wheel on a revolving hard plastic disc.

10 The "apprentice" or transferrer's assistant 'rubs down' the print using a stiff-bristled brush lubricated with soft soap to avoid the print becoming torn.
(The apron is a piece of printer's discarded felt from a roller.)

5 The Willow Pattern

UNA DES FONTAINES, writing about the *Early Printed Patterns at Etruria,* observes that Josiah Bateman, chief traveller of Wedgwood, wrote to his employer on 8 September 1817, in reply to a request for his opinion concerning the most suitable design to engrave for a Table service:

'I think a light pleasing Landscape would be preferable to anything Tonny Oriental – Country people do not understand anything about Pagodas or Chinese Temples – the Broseley pattern in Tea ware would do well – The reason I would recommend it – all printed China in blue is the same pattern, and that pattern in your ware (done faint) would look as well. It is so much approved by the country people that no other pattern blue printed China will go down, but it is for no other reason except that every (one) has it.'

Una des Fontaines illustrates this undiscriminating attitude by a typical order dated June 1824:

'It must be blue willow in any pattern.'[I]

The Willow pattern has retained this popularity, even though the romantic legend attaching to it is quite apocryphal.[II]

The main value of the legend is in identifying the principal features of the only design which should be called the Willow Pattern: the bridge with three persons crossing it, the willow tree, the boat, the main tea house, the two birds, and a fence across the foreground of the garden.[103]

This design was developed by Josiah Spode from an original Chinese pattern, called Mandarin. There is an earlier and more faithful version by Caughley, which Geoffrey Godden calls Willow-Nankin. (Fig. 1) He stresses, however, that Caughley never made the standard Willow pattern.[69] Certainly Josiah Spode I was the first potter in Staffordshire to copy the Chinese Mandarin design as shown in figure 2.

It also seems likely that Spode originated the Willow pattern, for those pieces with the coarse engraving and dark colour typical of the 1790s – the earliest Willow pieces – are of Spode manufacture. As to the design, a shard of Chinese porcelain (Fig. 3) excavated on the Spode factory in 1969 shows the form that inspired the tea house and a Chinese bowl is known (Fig. 4) which shows a bridge with three figures on it, though the rest of the design does not follow Willow pattern. The other elements in the design Spode would have built up from his familiarity with the Chinese originals of which he was supplying matchings or replacements.

The fence, for example, was a common enough Chinese motif that helped to balance the composition. As to the Willow tree itself, *salix buddleia populus,* the most likely model, is found in all parts of China. In Buddhist iconography the willow symbolises meekness, and as a symbol of spring, and for its characteristic suppleness and grace has come to represent woman also. The orange tree, which should bloom all year round, is regarded as a bringer of good luck, and plants are often given as gifts at the Lunar New Year.[III] Both trees are found represented on Chinese pottery.

Spode's first version of the Willow pattern may have been produced in about 1790. (Figs. 5 and 6) The engraving was all by line, except for the oranges on the tree, while the blue in which it was printed was quite dark, though bright and clear. Examples are rare. Leonard Whiter in his book *Spode,* distinguished the different versions of Willow by giving them subsidiary numbers, so that this version was called Willow, First, or Willow I: this system of nomenclature will be followed here.

Spode's Willow, Second, or Willow II, is from copper plates engraved at much the same period, all line work but of finer quality. The tone of blue

1. Group of ware Artificial porcelain. Blue printed in the pattern called by Godden 'Willow-Nankin' S (Caughley) mark. *Photo by courtesy of Geoffrey Godden, Chinaman.*

3. (*above*) **Shard of Chinese porcelain** showing the pillared front of a house from which that in the Willow pattern could have been developed. Excavated on the Spode factory, 1969.

2. (*top right*) **Stand** 22.1cm. Pearlware. Spode's Mandarin pattern.

4. (*right*) **Footed Bowl** *d.* 26.0cm. Chinese porcelain. Painted in blue with a landscape scene which includes a bridge with three persons on it, similar to that featured in the Willow pattern.

is paler and softer, a quality which is preferable to the later versions. (Fig. 7)

Willow, Third, or Willow III, was produced from newly engraved copper plates possibly after 1810; there are substantial areas of stipple punchwork, especially in the garden. In this version, which became the standard Willow Pattern, the colour varies from bright, clear blue in the earlier wares of 1810-1820, to the harder, non-flowing blue of the pieces which are commonly associated with the pattern. (Figs. 8 and 9)

There is, apparently, no Chinese pattern that contains all the features of the standard Willow pattern, and though there seems no doubt that the pattern was Spode's invention from Chinese originals, the expression has been loosely used even since the eighteenth century, for example on a bill from the London pottery and glass sellers Elizabeth North and Son, dated April 1799, which lists a sale of tea ware printed in 'brown edge Willow'.[103] It is this inaccuracy that may have led some writers to ascribe its origin elsewhere,

5. Round fluted dessert dish Scalloped edge, *d.* 22.6cm. Pearlware. Printed in Dark Royal 1 1 0, from an almost totally line-engraved copper plate. Spode's Willow I.

SPODE ৪

SPODE

6. Supper section 32.0cm. *l.* Pearlware. Printed in Dark Royal 1 1 0, and in blue. Spode's Willow I.

SPODE /

7. Plate *d.* 20.8cm.
Pearlware. Printed in
Royal 1 1 0, from a
copper more finely
engraved than that used
for Willow I. Spode's
Willow II.

COPELAND
& GARRETT

8. Hot water plate *d.*
24.6cm. Pearlware, with
embossed rose as plug.
Printed in bright Royal
1 1 0, hard with no flow.
Spode's Willow III.

SPODE

9. Hot water plate *d.* 29.9cm overall. Pearlware. Printed in bright Royal 1 1 0, clearer and harder with less flow of the colour. Much stipple punchwork.

10. Print on paper from a Spode copper engraving *c.* 1800. Notice the extensive use of line-work. Only the orange tree and fir tree (top left) seem to be stipple punched. *Courtesy Spode Limited Museum.*

11. Print on paper from a twentieth century engraving. The whole effect is coarser than the earlier one.

particularly to Thomas Turner and Thomas Minton at Caughley.[25] It is true, as Shaw states,[154] that Turner created the 'first Blue Printed Table Service made in England, for Whitmore Esq., father of the present Member for Bridgnorth. The pattern was called Nankin and had much similarity to the Broseley Tea Pattern' which Minton helped to design. Perhaps the names were confused. However, Geoffrey Godden's research shows that the name 'Willow' is not applied to any pattern in the Caughley records, and the Caughley Rag Book, which contains prints from their engraved copper plates, does not contain a design with all the features of Willow, though it does contain other chinoiserie designs.[IV]

Figures 10 and 11 show Spode Willow patterns from the eighteenth century and the present. These have all the features of the standard design, which are the willow tree in the centre, leaning over the bridge, the tea house with three pillars forming the portico and a large orange tree behind it. The bridge should have three figures crossing towards the island, and on the lake there is a boat with a man in it. Two birds flying towards each other form the top centre, and a fence crosses the foreground. The border and nankin are also distinctive, although they may not appear on some smaller pieces, and the border is common to another Spode pattern.

A number of other manufacturers produced Willow pattern over the years, and some of these are illustrated (Figs. 12 to 26) along with Spode designs. There are no sure guides to the attribution of pieces, or to their dating. The number of arches on the bridge is not an indication of the maker, for example (some of Spode's designs have three, others five). Another such fallible guideline is the number of oranges on the tree. Both these quantities vary and depend on the size of the piece being printed, a dinner plate requiring a different arrangement from a cup or saucer, for example. The strength of the blue print may be some guide to age, but the quality of the print must be correctly interpreted. Very early prints could be dark Cyanine or midnight blues, when the colour often flowed slightly. As the technology and experience of the potter improved, so the blues, both in the mixing and in the glost firing were better controlled. Medium toned blues such as royal and ultramarine blue were popular until the second decade of the nineteenth century when paler colours became fashionable. In Victorian times a whole variety of blues were produced, ranging from grey blues to dark flow-blues in which it is hard to discern the basic pattern.[V] The continuous popularity of Willow Pattern makes the study of it a study of the changes in design standards, colour fashions and pottery bodies.

CHAPTER FIVE: NOTES

I   I am very grateful to Mrs des Fontaines[50] for this quotation which might have provided the title to this book!
II   The author must here record his thanks in particular to Phyllis Edwards and Dr Edmund Launert, who have tried to identify the different botanical species shown on Chinese landscape designs. Unfortunately, the liberties of the artists, both Chinese and British, are such as to make firm identification misleading and impossible.
III   It has even been suggested that Thomas Turner copied the designs from a French piece, and further invented the legend to cover up!
IV   See the discussion and illustration of different blues on page 79.

12. Stand with pierced border, 25.4cm. *l.*
Pearlware. Printed in Royal 1 1 0, with hand
painting added as shading to the bottom of the
centre design. Blue crown mark, probably Spode.

13. Meat dish 53.2cm *l.* Pearlware. Printed in
Royal 1 1 0. Large C mark in blue. *Cresswell
Antiques, Tittensor, Staffs.*

14. Meat dish 39.3cm. *l.* Pearlware. Printed in
Royal 1 1 0. The back combed and glazed.
Unmarked. *Cresswell Antiques.*

15. Meat dish 44.9cm. *l.* Pearlware. Printed in pale Royal 1 1 0. Note the five arches. Blue and impressed marks. *Cresswell Antiques.*

16. Meat dish 47.0cm. *l.* Pearlware. Printed in pale Royal 1 1 0. The back combed and glazed. Unmarked. *Cresswell Antiques.*

19. Dish 48.1cm. *l.* Pearlware. Printed in Ultramarine, 1 0 8. Marks, impressed R O G E R S &, in blue, 2. *Cresswell Antiques.*

17. Plate *d*. 25.2 cm. Pearlware. Printed in Cyanine 105. The border is similar to that usually found on 'Long Bridge' pattern. Notice that the third person on the bridge has turned back. Unmarked.

18. Plate *d*. 23.2 cm. Pearlware. Printed in Cyanine 105. Very fine line engraving in the garden area. Triangular mark in blue.

20. Dish 47.8 cm. *l*. Pearlware. Printed in Royal 110. Workman's mark in blue.

21. Dish 44.6cm. *l*. White earthenware. Printed in very pale Cyanine 1 0 5. Marks, impressed and printed: STONEWARE PW & Co. *Cresswell Antiques.*

22. Dish 52.3cm. *l*. Pearlware. Printed in Royal 1 1 0. Mark, very faint and blurred, in blue.

23. Dish 56.0cm. *l*. Pearlware. Printed in Ultramarine 1 0 8, combed base. Mark R. & C. in blue. *Cresswell Antiques.*

SPODE ∿

24. Dish 42.4cm. *l.* Pearlware. Printed in Royal 1 1 0.

25. Dish 48.9cm. *l.* Earthenware. Printed in blue underglaze. Mark H E R C U L A N E U M impressed, *c.* 1815. *Photo: The City of Liverpool Museum.*

SPODE

26. Dish 23.5cm. *l.* Earthenware. Printed in blue, with edge painted with lustre. Probably intended for serving potted char.

6 Mandarin and Rock Patterns

MANDARIN AND Rock are considered immediately following Willow Pattern because they bear a strong resemblance to it, and indeed Mandarin seems to have been the origin for it.

The principal features of Mandarin pattern are the central willow tree growing at the edge of a river and leaning out to the left over the water, the tea house to the right of the scene, with a smaller pavilion to its left, two birds flying and an island at the top left, with a boat propelled by a man with a pole. A large orange tree usually grows behind the tea house. The general appearance resembles that of the Willow pattern, but certain details differ: there is no bridge and no fence, the fronts of the tea house and pavilion are different, and several of the trees at the right of the buildings are dissimilar. This was one of the favourite patterns imported into Europe in the eighteenth century and many of the porcelain factories in Ching-tê-Chên must have produced it, and, because it was hand painted, there are many variations of a minor sort.[94] The first English pottery to reproduce it as a transfer print was Caughley, a print in the factory rag book (Fig. 1) showing the centre design for an oval dish. Godden's photograph of two soup tureens[68] (Fig. 2), comparing the Chinese on the left with the Caughley/Coalport on the right, shows how close the early copies were, including the attempt to reproduce the effect of shaded washes of colour in the garden. But the borders are not those usually found with this pattern, which Godden calls Willow-Nankin. (Fig. 3)

Spode probably was the second to copy this pattern, which he did quite faithfully. After nearly two hundred years, it is not possible to say which Chinese variation he was asked to copy, but the several Chinese examples which can be compared to Spode's earthenware (Figs. 4 and 5) are not very different, except in one respect – the nankin design. Instead of the double or single honeycomb pattern, Spode used the nankin that he later adopted for Willow Pattern (Fig. 6). Both these Spode earthenware pieces are in Cyanine blue, and engraved. The pearlware slop basin (Fig. 7) is of unproven origin. The border inside is the same as the nankin used by Spode, while the details and quality also suggest that it might be by Spode, but the shape is unusual. Inside there is a ridge as well as on the outside which is fluted only at the top, the remainder having been shaved off by the turner. Other items of teaware with this feature have been seen, but none marked with a manufacturer's name (Fig. 8). When Spode introduced his bone china about 1799, this pattern may have been one of the first which he used.[203]

Not only did Spode not allocate pattern numbers to pieces made as matchings for Chinese originals, but it also seems that the pattern records were not kept in an orderly fashion until Henry Daniel started working for Spode in about 1802.[82] The patterns were recorded only when some decoration was added over the glaze and subsequently fired through the enamel kiln. So even the pattern when used with gold edging on bone china is unnumbered and cannot be exactly dated. A variant is illustrated in figure 9.

Spode omitted the orange tree, enlarged the willow tree and relocated the boat, but the trellis border with dagger bead, characteristic of the Chinese wares (Fig. 10) was now adopted. It is this border which suggested to Whiter the name Dagger-Landscape, but as the name Mandarin is so well established on the Spode factory it will be used here to designate this pattern. The various forms which vary slightly among one another according to the pottery body can be numbered as follows: Mandarin I, on pearlware, Mandarin II on

1. Print on cloth Caughley rag book No. 120.

2. Comparison of a Chinese true porcelain soup tureen (left) with one in artificial porcelain by Caughley/Coalport, shown with a fragment from the Caughley site. *Photo by courtesy of Geoffrey Godden, Chinaman.*

3. Plate *d*. 18.2cm. Porcelain. Printed in Cyanine 1 0 5. Unmarked. Attributed to Caughley.

4 Round plate *d*. 24.0cm. Chinese porcelain. Painted in blue.

5. Teapot 23.0cm. *l*. Chinese porcelain. Painted in blue, and richly gilded.

6. (*right*) **Covered sugar bowl** 13.5cm. *h*. Pearlware. Printed in blue with gilded knob, bands and handle-rings & foot. Mandarin I pattern. Workman's mark in blue. Attributed to Spode 1795-1800.

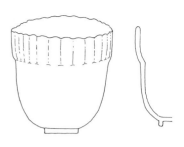

7. (*left*) **Slop basin** *d*. 15.5cm. Pearlware. Printed in blue with ocre edge. Note ridge on outside.

8. (*above*) **Drawing** of cup shape.

9. Saucer Bone china. Printed in bright Ultramarine 1 0 8, with gilded edge. Mandarin II pattern, *c*. 1800.

10. Saucer *d*. 12.5cm. Chinese porcelain. Painted in Royal 1 1 0, with gilded edge.

bone china and Mandarin III on stone china.

The version on stone china (Fig. 11) is on the Royal Flute shape; a teacup of this shape, undecorated, is recorded in the pattern books as number 619, datable to about 1804.[1]

Several versions by other manufacturers are known. One (Fig. 12) with trellis border and honeycomb nankin, has a centre which seems to

have been 'interpreted', that is, changed from the Chinese into something more fanciful. The stem of the willow tree is intertwined and the botanical species have been varied. The orange tree is taller and there are more, but smaller fruits. The buildings are changed, and no birds fly in the sky. A twenty-inch dish is known with the 'daisy star' mark. Another earthenware plate (Fig. 13), with a

11. Saucer *d*. 14.0cm tea cup *d*. 8.85cm. Coffee can. 6.5cm. *h*. Stone china.
Printed in blue, with finely gilded bead below border, gilded edge and lines.
Mandarin III pattern. Royal Flute shape, with Bute handle. 1813-15.

12. Plate *d*. 25.3cm. Pearlware. Printed in blue. No
marks.

13. Plate *d*. 24.7cm. Earthenware. Printed in
Ultramarine 1 0 8: no foot, rounded bottom. Mark B,
incised.

border something like that of Long Bridge, and a willow pattern nankin, demonstrates all the main features of the pattern in the centre, even if the border is unusual.[II]

The Mandarin Pattern continued to be produced by the Spode factory until the 1950s on earthenware as plain prints in either pink or Nanking blue. In the early years of this century it was made on bone china especially as coffee ware in the same Nanking blue.

At first glance, the Rock Pattern can be mistaken for Mandarin, but there are many differences, amongst which the most important are that the willow tree has but two or three main branches with leaves, instead of four, there is a walla walla or canopied boat in which are two persons one of whom is playing a flute, and there is only one main building, a tea house, with a hut at the extreme right. A dominant line of rocks in the foreground distinguishes the pattern and gives it its name. The small hut on the island is of an unusual type, characteristic of those built to protect the grain once it has been harvested, and the birds in the pattern are depicted differently from those on the Mandarin Pattern.

The Chinese porcelain saucer (Fig. 14) was copied by Caughley, a record of which occurs as number 51 in the rag book (Fig. 15). Though Godden[63] considers this to be a version of the Willow-Nankin (Mandarin) pattern, the differences are wide enough to justify the different name, and the Chinese wares employ borders which are quite distinct from Mandarin.

Spode's first variation, Rock I (Fig. 16), occurs on pearlware and is of a pre-1800 date. The engraving, by line-work, copies a Chinese piece similar to that in figure 17. The border copies only some of the Chinese features, however, an exact match being as yet unknown. This border was used also by Spode for the Forest-Landscape pattern. A covered sugar box of Old Oval Shape (Fig. 18) is another early piece which is pearlware and gilded.

Spode also made a second variation on bone china, Rock II (Fig. 19), in which he copied a Chinese piece which has a border containing Y-work. The Spode plate seems to have been printed from a smaller engraving than the centre area, because there are hand-painted lines and shading to the left; perhaps indicating that it was a special order for someone who found the pearl-ware version an insufficiently good match.

Apart from the Caughley and Spode copies the only other manufacturer's version (Fig. 20) is a plate, the design of which embodies the principal features of the Chinese, but the border is different from all those reviewed here. It does reflect the Chinese idiom, however, and might have been a copy. This piece is printed with the 'leafy spray' mark.

An interesting item (Fig. 21) which might be either Rock or Forest-Landscape is the butter dish with fixed stand, perhaps made for serving asparagus. The similarity of the handle to that of the sugar box in figure 18 suggests that this is a Spode piece, as well as the fact that the border has not been seen on other manufacturers' wares.

CHAPTER SIX: NOTES

I   These pieces have been found since Whiter's statement that the pattern is only found on bone china.[204]
II   Other wares in this design included a Maling (Newcastle on Tyne) tea cup and saucer of about 1902, illustrated by Bell,[15] who also shows an oval dish dated 1897. Godden illustrates a teapot inscribed S. Tonill, 1789.

14. Saucer *d*. 12.8cm. Chinese porcelain. Painted in Cyanine 1 0 5 with ocre edge.

16. Plate *d.* 20.5cm. Pearlware. Printed in Royal 1 1 0. Rock I. 1795-1800.

15. Print on cloth Caughley rag book, No. 51.

17. Round plate *d.* 25.6cm. Chinese porcelain. Painted in Royal, 1 1 0.

18. Sugar box Old Oval shape, *l.* 14.4cm. Pearlware. Printed in Royal 1 1 0, and gilded. Rock I. 1795-1800.   SPODE

19. Plate *d*. 22.0cm. Bone china. Printed in bright Ultramarine 1 0 8, with painted additions. Probably intended as a matching. Rock II. 1800-1810.

20. Round plate *d*. 20.0cm. Pearlware. Printed in blue. Mark of a spray of leaves.

21. Asparagus butter dish *l*. 22.0cm. Pearlware. No mark. Attributed to Spode.

7 Two Temples Pattern

TWO TEMPLES PATTERN was, after the Willow and Mandarin patterns, one of the most widely copied of Chinese landscape designs, and many Chinese originals are known which differ only in detail. Each English factory probably referred to its own version by a specific name or number, which may have been that used by a competitor. A few of these names are recorded in lists of copper engravings, pattern books and account books. For example, the Minton Inventory of 1810 lists the following names in the catalogue of copper plates: Willow, China Pattern, NaKing Tea & Toyset, Pagoda, Red House, Trophy, Chinese Temple, Broseley. Geoffrey Godden also notes that the name Pagoda 'occurs in the contemporary Chamberlain (Worcester) accounts'.[24] In fact this pattern illustrates better than most the problems of nomenclature, the more so because the common name Pagoda is based on a misinterpretation of the main element in the design.

1. Plate *d*. 21.3 cm. Chinese porcelain (1780-1800). Painted in Royal 1 1 0, with gilded edge and bead, added in England, possibly by Miles Mason.

Figure 1, a Chinese porcelain plate, shows clearly the basic features; they can be traced on an unmarked Caughley porcelain saucer (Fig. 2) and, less accurately copied, on a Spode soup plate (Fig. 3).(The Spode name for this pattern was Temple.) The main features of the pattern are the building, a bridge with two people on it, the fence, apparently crossing the river, and a willow tree. The building has given rise to the name Pagoda, but in fact it is not one building but two temples, one in front of the other[1] (Fig. 4). This confusion perhaps arose because of the different Oriental system of perspective, and indeed some Chinese pieces and some English versions also, show the overlap more clearly. Two Temples is therefore a more appropriate name than Pagoda, but it does not appear that any manufacturer used the name. The suggestion is therefore that patterns be described as Two Temples together with the manufacturer's name and the manufacturer's title, if that is known. For example, Spode's Two Temples II, variation Broseley, or Davenport's Two Temples II.

Figures 5 to 15 show other Chinese originals and various manufacturers' versions. The differences in the patterns are slight; in some the bridge has a straight parapet, others a curved one, in some the two temples are more closely aligned than in others, the river seems to flow up to the temple gates in some but not all, and so on. One

2. Saucer *d*. 13.2 cm. Porcelain. Printed in Royal 1 1 0, with gilded edge. No mark. (Caughley 1780-90).

3. Soup plate *d.* 20.4cm. Bone china.
Printed in Ultramarine 108, with gilded
edge. *c.* 1809.

6. Coffee cup and saucer Chinese porcelain (1780-
1800). Painted in Cyanine 1 0 5.

5. Oval dish 28.5cm. *l.* Pearlware. Printed in Ultramarine 1 0 8. Centre area
raised. Mark SEMI-CHINA WARRANTED.

4. Sketch of design of two Temples.

7. Soup plate *d*. 16.5cm. Chinese porcelain. Painted in Royal 1 1 0. (1780-1800).

9. (*right*) **Tea cup and saucer.** Porcelain. Printed in Cyanine 1 0 5, with gilded edge. Mark S (Caughley 1780-90). The ornamental gable end has a petal-like edge.

8. Teapot and covered sugar box Teapot 14cm *h*. Earthenware. Printed in blue and gilded. Possibly by Minton.

10. Plate *d.* 19.2 cm. Bone china. Printed in pale Ultramarine 1 0 8. Unmarked.

11. Plate *d.* 19.9 cm. Porcelain. Printed in Smalt 1 6 6. Mark Grainger & Co Worcester (1805-12).

12. Tea cup and saucer *d.* 14.4 cm. Bone china. Printed in pale Ultramarine 1 0 8, with gilded bead and edge. Mark S J R in box border.

13. Tea cup, fluted, *d.* 9.4 cm. Pearlware. Printed in Royal 1 1 0, gilded edge and foot line. Unmarked. **Coffee can** *d.* 6.3 cm. Bone china. **Tea cup**, *d.* 8.7 cm. Bone china. Printed in Royal 1 1 0.

14. Plate *d.* 25.7 cm. White earthenware. Printed in pale Cyanine 1 0 5. Traces of a gilded edge, and band on the shoulder. Davenport anchor mark impressed, with the impresed registration mark for Mar. 13, 1879, and DAVENPORT printed in blue, 3109 in red, and a cross in green.

15. Cream jug 13.2 cm. *l.* Porcelain or bone china, heavily stained. Printed in pale Ultramarine 1 0 8. Possibly Miles Mason.

difference is important. Spode's Two Temples variation Temple contains four figures, two on the bridge, one in the temple doorway and a fourth standing on the rocks in front of the temple. Spode also produced a version called Broseley, which omits the fourth figure. This pattern is found on bone china only on teawares, usually

printed in pale ultramarine blue. Figures 16 to 20 show examples from Spode, and figures 21 and 22 Miles Mason's version.[II] Caughley's version is seen in figure 7.

The absence of the fourth figure is not the only distinction, for the borders (see Figs. 23 and 24) used on each also vary. In the Temple border, the panel of lattice work (a in Fig. 23) contains three or four complete lozenge shapes, the space between them and the rim being filled with a sunburst design. The butterfly symbol (b) is accompanied by a partial daisy emblem on the rim. Between these two items is a panel (c) containing two partial daisy emblems. On the Broseley border (Fig. 24) the panel is filled with uniform lattice-work; the butterfly design (b) goes up to the rim and the single daisy emblem in the intervening panel (c) has two branches to it.

The fact that the different borders are each accompanied by a different centre design suggests that there are properly two versions of Two Temples pattern, version I being Spode's Temple pattern, version II Broseley, which was probably produced at a later date.[III] This nomenclature has been followed here: for example, the Caughley patterns in figures 2 and 25 are Two Temples I, and that in figure 9 is Two Temples II, as the title Pagoda, though a Caughley factory name, cannot be ascribed with certainty to either.

Because Spode used the Two Temples pattern frequently on teawares it was often gilded. Figures 26 to 32 show a selection of designs from the Spode pattern book for such ornamentation.[IV] The desired pattern, Temple or Broseley, is also marked in most cases.

CHAPTER SEVEN: NOTES

I Cyril Williams Wood, in his article *When Underglaze Printing was a Secret Technique*, first drew attention to the misnomer and suggested the title Two Temples.[212]
II The shards excavated on the Islington factory,[162] here illustrated by permission of Alan Smith (Figs. 33,34) are particularly interesting in view of Miles Mason's work there.
III Spode pattern numbers add weight to this supposition. Temple appears earliest as no. 1481 (circa 1810) and Broseley as 2892 (circa 1819), even though this date may be later than its introduction as a plain blue print.
IV Other factories known to have added gilded borders include Miles Mason and Rockingham.

16. Plate *d.* 20.4cm. Bone china. Printed in pale Ultramarine 1 0 8, with gilded edge. Notice how the nearer temple is to the left of the further one, and there is no man in the garden.

20. Plate *d.* 18.7cm. Earthenware. Printed in pale Ultramarine 1 0 8. (1818-25). 𝕾𝕻𝕺𝕯𝕰

17. Tea cup and saucer; saucer *d.* 14.1cm. Bone china. Printed in pale Ultramarine 1 0 8, with gilded edge. 1818-25. London shape. SPODE

18. Teapot and plate. Teapot, 11.4cm. *h.*, plate, *d.* 18.2cm. Bone china. Printed in pale Ultramarine 1 0 8, with gilding. Round, Sweep Neck Teapot shape (1818-20).

SPODE

19. Cream jug and sugar box. Jug 13.3cm *l.* sugar box, 18.2cm. *l.* Bone china, printed in pale Ultramarine and gilded. New oval shape, *c.* 1819.

SPODE

21. Saucer d. 14.0cm. Porcelain. Printed in Royal/Arabian, 110/104, with gilded edge. Two Temples I. The foot is wiped clear of glaze and has turned brown (as found in Chinese porcelain). No mark. Probably Miles Mason.

22. Saucer d. 14.5cm. Bone china. Printed in Ultramarine 108. Attributed to Miles Mason (1804-12).

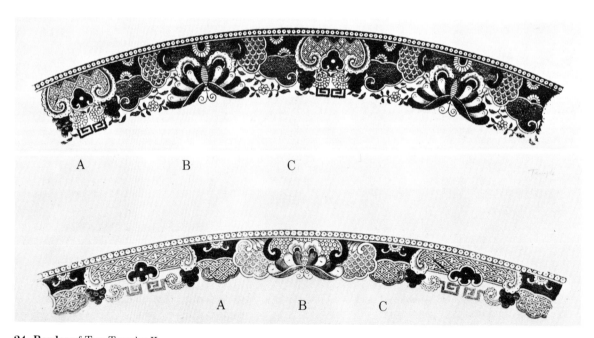

24. Border of Two Temples II.

22. A mark on the underside of the saucer in Figure 22.

25. Print on cloth. Caughley Rag Book No. 89 showing water reaching the temple gates.
Centre of Two Temples I.

26 to **32**
A selection of illustrations from the Spode pattern books recording gilded ornamentation applied to cups with the various Two Temples patterns.
Reproduced by courtesy of Spode Ltd.

TWO TEMPLES

Print from engraved copper plate of Spode's 'Temple'.
(by kind permission of Spode Limited)

This analytical chart illustrates the principal features on only *six* different examples of the Two Temples pattern. The drawings are not to scale; they are more like sketches which are intended to serve as quick reference points rather than exact copies.

Similar charts might be prepared by collectors of their objects in this pattern, using the reference numbers given here as universal reference points. Variations in the border designs are discussed on pages , and attribution seems unlikely to be helped much by further detailed analysis.

Pattern		Two Temples I var. 'Te
Maker		Spode
Object analysed		Soup plate 20.6 cm.
1	Roof tiling	solid strip
2	Gable end	
3	Windows	
4	Roof tiling	vertical stripes
5	Steps to Temple	
6	Bridge	curve para
6a	Figures on bridge	
7	Fence in foreground	stra solid hand
8	Willow tree	Yes
9	Willow tree	None by bridge
10	Fence by bridge	Solid handra
11	Figure by steps	Yes: facing left
12	Sampan	Double shade
13	Bridge on island	
14	Huts	well made, unadorne
14a	Temple	Pagoda type
15	Windows in wall	
16	Man in doorway	faces left desk: doub 'rim' to door
17	Grass	line engraved
18	Pinnacle	
19a	Ridge designs	
19b		
19c		
19d		
Body		Bone china
Marks		SPODE printed
Colour		Ultramarine 108

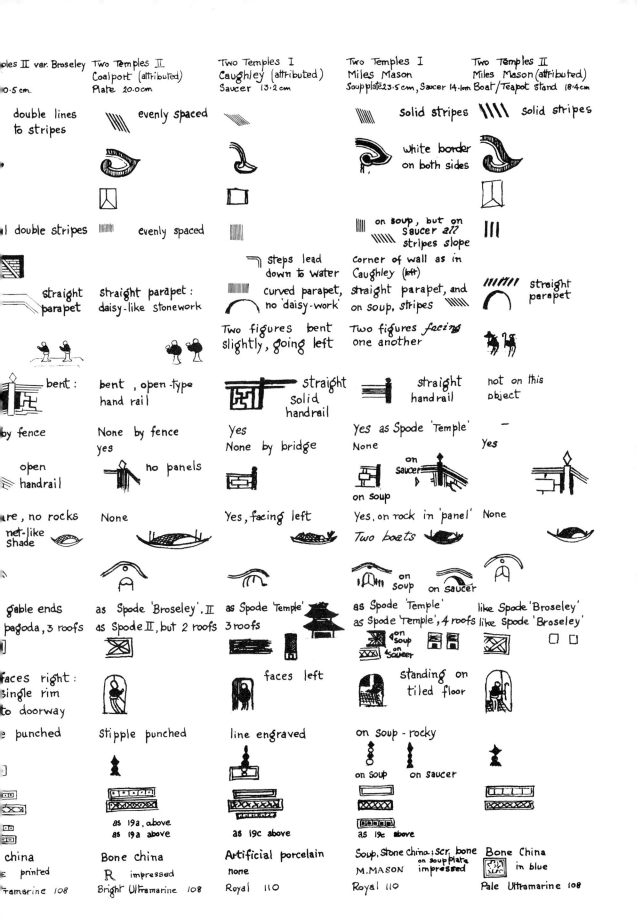

...ples II var. Broseley 0.5 cm.	Two Temples II Coalport (attributed) Plate 20.0 cm	Two Temples I Caughley (attributed) Saucer 13.2 cm	Two Temples I Miles Mason Soup plate 23.5 cm, Saucer 14.1 cm	Two Temples II Miles Mason (attributed) Boat/Teapot stand 18.4 cm
double lines to stripes	evenly spaced		solid stripes	solid stripes
			white border on both sides	
double stripes	evenly spaced		on soup, but on saucer all stripes slope	
straight parapet	straight parapet: daisy-like stonework	steps lead down to water; curved parapet, no 'daisy-work'	corner of wall as in Caughley (left); straight parapet, and on soup, stripes	straight parapet
		Two figures bent slightly, going left	Two figures facing one another	
bent:	bent, open-type hand rail	straight solid handrail	straight handrail	not on this object
by fence	None by fence / yes	Yes / None by bridge	Yes as Spode 'Temple' / None	Yes / —
open handrail	no panels		on saucer / on soup	
...re, no rocks net-like shade	None	Yes, facing left	Yes, on rock in 'panel' / Two boats	None
			on soup / on saucer	
gable ends, pagoda, 3 roofs	as Spode 'Broseley'. II / as Spode II, but 2 roofs	as Spode 'Temple' / 3 roofs	as Spode 'Temple' / as Spode 'Temple', 4 roofs; on soup, on saucer	like Spode 'Broseley' / like Spode 'Broseley'
faces right: single rim to doorway		faces left	standing on tiled floor	
punched	Stipple punched	line engraved	on soup - rocky; on soup / on saucer	
	as 19a, above / as 19a above	as 19c above	as 19c above	
china printed; ...ramarine 108	Bone china; R impressed; Bright Ultramarine 108	Artificial porcelain; none; Royal 110	Soup, Stone china; scr. bone; on soup plate; M.MASON impressed; Royal 110	Bone China; in blue; Pale Ultramarine 108

30   31   32

33. Biscuit fragments. Porcelain. Printed in blue, with the open areas washed-in by hand with blue. Note trellis border and gilded decoration below on right saucer fragment. *Photo: Alan Smith.*

34. Biscuit fragments. Porcelain. Left, unhandled tea cup; right, teacup. Both printed in blue and hardened on. *Photo: Alan Smith.*

35. Plate *d.* 21.0cm. Pearlware. Printed in pale Royal 1 1 0. Mark Don Pottery in blue 1820-24.

36. Plate *d.* 25.5cm. White earthenware. Printed in Royal 1 1 0. Attributed to W. Mason (1813-20).

37. Handled plate 23.7cm. *l.* Bone china. Printed in pale Ultramarine 1 0 8, with gilded edge. H.G. mark in blue.

38. Plate *d.* 18.4cm. Pearlware. Printed in pale blue. Marks WEDGWOOD impressed, and X in blue *c.* 1817.

39. Tea cup and saucer (saucer *d.* 14.1cm.) Bone china. Printed in pale Ultramarine 1 0 8. Unmarked. Two Temples I, possibly Minton.

40. Teapot 27.0cm. *l.* Porcelain or bone china. Printed in pale Ultramarine 1 0 8, with gilding. Unmarked. The shape is like the 'canoe' shape of Miles Mason.

41. Tea cup and saucer (saucer *d.* 14.0cm.) Bone china. Printed in Royal 1 1 0. Marks on cup and on saucer.

8 Early reproductions of Chinese landscapes

THE PATTERNS Two Figures and Pearl River House exhibit characteristics which suggest that they were the earliest produced by Josiah Spode I by the underglaze transfer printing process in the years 1785-90.

For years this pattern, named Two Figures by Leonard Whiter, seemed to be an adaptation of two patterns made by Caughley. Features from patterns called by Godden Conversation and Full-Nankin, occur in Two Figures, especially the border which is almost an exact copy of that used with Full-Nankin. But in 1977 a tea cup and saucer of exactly this Two Figures pattern came to light. It was made of Chinese porcelain (Fig. 1). In the same way, the Caughley Full Nankin pattern (Fig. 2) has a Chinese prototype (Fig. 3), and there is probably a Chinese prototype for the Conversation pattern illustrated here with a print in the Caughley rag book (Fig. 4).

All these patterns are early – the blues are dark and the line engraving is coarse with no light and shade: the engraver adopted the style of the woodcut. They must be amongst the first ever produced for hot printing in blue, and surely fit the description by Simeon Shaw[156] 'The (copper) Plates were so extremely strong that no delicate shades were preserved. The specimens have scarcely anything deserving the name of a *fine part*'.

The principal features of this pattern are a central white area in which two figures greet each other, a single tea house behind these figures, and a straight-parapet bridge on the left with one man on the right end of it looking as if he is awaiting a guest. A sampan (often of exceptionally slender shape) is in the immediate foreground. There is a willow tree, but a very small one on the island to the left which is not very important.[1]

The Chinese version (Fig. 1) shows the man on

1. Saucer Fluted shape, *d.* 12.8cm. Chinese porcelain. Painted in Cyanine 1 0 5, with traces on the edge of metallic gold, the stain of the fixing medium still evident. Original of Two Figures I.

the bridge carrying a crooked stick, and the sampan is very much of the usual type – that is one for work rather than for pleasure. An extremely early Spode stand with pierced border (Fig. 5) has copied the Chinese fairly faithfully, but the man is on the top of the bridge, while the sampan is closer to it than usual. Another early Spode stand (Fig. 6) shows some refinement and a much closer appearance to the more common Spode example (Fig. 7).

One characteristic mark of Spode's pattern is the nicely engraved nankin of honeycomb design: this is of regular hexagons, the spaces between are not too big, and the lines within the hexagons taper slightly to the centre. This honeycomb

2. Oval dish 40.6 cm. *l.* Porcelain. Printed in dark blue, with the pattern called Full Nankin. Unmarked (Caughley) *Photo: Geoffrey Godden – Chinaman.*

3. Octagonal dish. Chinese porcelain. Painted in dark blue. *Photo: Geoffrey Godden – Chinaman.*

SPODE

6. Pierced Stand 27.7 cm. *l.* Pearlware. Printed in Cyanine 105. An early form of Two Figures II.

4. Print on cloth from the Caughley Rag
Book (no. 45) Conversation pattern.

7. Plate *d.* 24.8cm. Pearlware. Printed
in dark Royal 1 1 0. The standard
version of Two Figures II.   SPODE

SPODE

5. Pierced stand 22.0cm. *l.* Pearlware.
Printed in Cyanine 1 0 5. This very early
version will be called Two Figures I.

nankin on the plate (Fig. 8) has flattened hexagons
and wider spaces between each. The nankin on
the Heath dish has a double line at the edge of
each hexagon, while the shading on the bridge
parapet slopes inwards, instead of being vertical
across the whole length of it.

Another version has a different border altogether.

A tea cup and saucer (Fig. 9) and an asparagus
tray (Fig. 10) share this characteristic. The border
is a continuous trellis design with a recumbent
silkworm bead below it.

A jug has yet another border (Fig. 11), very
similar to the Chinese design (Fig. 1) and to an old
copper engraving in the Spode collection (Fig.

8. Plate *d.* 24.9cm. Pearlware. Printed in dark blue which has *flown* in the glost firing. No marks. Three single dottle marks below rim.

11. Handled jug, or pitcher 16.2cm *h*. Pearlware. Printed in Royal 1 1 0. No marks.

9. Tea cup and saucer. Cup *d.* 8.3cm, saucer *d.* 12.8cm. Pearlware. Printed in Royal 1 1 0, with gilded edge, and recumbent silkworm bead below the trellis border. The shape has a slight ridge inside, and is fluted. Workmen's marks on each.

10. Asparagus dish 28.2 cm. *l*. Pearlware. Printed in dark Cyanine 1 0 5. Unmarked. Broadly line engraved with trellis border and recumbent silkworm bead.

12. Print on paper from an engraving in the Spode factory collection. Although superficially appearing the same as the border on the jug, a careful comparison will reveal many differences of detail.

13. Tea cup d. 9.2cm. Pearlware. Printed Royal/Cyanine 110/105. Mark in blue. Note border and ridged shape.

14. Dessert dish d. 20.6cm. Pearlware, pressed with 'rush' foot. Printed in Cyanine 105, with sprays also on the reverse.

12), but it is not identical. A cup (Fig. 13) of the type with a ridge inside and fluting at the top only, is of this same variety. A shell shaped dessert comport (Fig. 14)[II] is marked with the eight-pointed 'daisy-star'. The upper gallery, or lantern, of the tea house in this example is quite different to that in the standard pattern, and other variances can be observed. Other examples in this Two Figures pattern are illustrated for interest.[III] (Figs. 15, 16, 17)

The Pearl River House pattern was almost unknown until 1974. In that year some broken shards were dug up on the Spode factory, to give a clear idea of the pattern, and a collector in Canada sent the author a photograph of an oval dish (Fig. 18) in this pattern, carrying the impressed Spode mark. Previously the only example to come to light had been a saucer which was unmarked though it looked like a Spode piece.

The main feature of the pattern is a house made of plaited palm leaf panels. It stands on the right of a bridge with a rounded arch and parapet. In front of the house is a short fence of large bamboo posts. There is no person or boat in the scene. The house seemed unlike those of the familiar Chinese style, so it was temporarily named Batavian Hut,

for it might have been intended for the Dutch East Indian market. When Dr Bernard Watney visited the Spode museum he said that New Hall had made it and that the bamboo feature had suggested the name Trench Mortar pattern.[189] A later suggested name, Malayan Village, was taken from the title of the illustration (Fig. 19) in T. & W. Daniell's *Picturesque Voyage to India by the Way of China,* published in 1810 . The pattern itself was probably not derived from this work, because the ware preceded it. It is now thought to represent a house on the banks of the Pearl River near to Canton, so the name Pearl River House is here used.

Several Chinese porcelain pieces are known[98] of which a coffee saucer (Fig. 20) is illustrated; the English varieties are certain to be intended as reproductions or replacements: examples known to have been made by New Hall[90] (Fig. 21), Spode (Figs. 22 to 24)[IV] and at least one other earthenware manufacturer (Fig. 25 and 26). Pearlware shards, excavated in Canada (Fig. 27) display minor differences from the foregoing, and a plate of pearlware which is different again, having a man fishing from a boat, two birds in the sky and other variations, is also known (Fig. 22).

The characteristics of the Spode version are three triangular-shaped hills, two bamboo stems between the bridge and the house, a tree *behind* the house and the carefully entwined gable ends of the roof coverings. This last feature is well illustrated on the fine coffee pot (Fig. 24).

CHAPTER EIGHT: NOTES

I Writers who have commented on the pattern include A.W. Coysh who implies,[34] mistakenly, that it was printed in underglaze blue on earthenware at Caughley in 1780. He states that 'copper plates of this design still exist with the initials TT (Thomas Turner) engraved in the margin'. I wonder if he is confusing it with the proven Caughley Conversation and Full Nankin patterns? Prints in the Rag Book are proof of these (i.e. Full Nankin and AGW/F4 Conversation). Stanley Harrison, when proprietor of the latter day Coalport factory, presented my father with the original engraving of Full Nankin. Coysh illustrates two examples of the Two Figures pattern: a plate, marked with a printed six-pointed star, and a dish with an impressed IH – the mark of Joshua Heath. Coysh draws attention to the addition of writing scrolls in the border of the dish, which do not appear on the plate; the border of Full Nankin pattern does include them. The plate seems to have been printed from the same engraving as Coysh's plate, though it is unmarked and with the centre in a different relationship to the border. Another dish (Fig. 23) illustrates Joshua Heath's version of the pattern.

II A very similar piece is illustrated by Morton Nance, and identified as Swansea (Plate XIII A).

III Lastly, a conundrum. I am told that there is no evidence to suggest that earthenware was manufactured by the Caughley factory. Although earthenware shards have been excavated,[77] they, along with other shards, were almost certainly imported to fill up holes, probably after the factory closed. The plate of Full Nankin pattern, is printed in blue on pearlware. It is engraved in the coarse style of Two Figures and is not so fine as the Caughley print on porcelain but at first glance it looks temptingly like it. It is certainly early, but its origin is not known. A soup plate with an almost identical print on pearlware is also known to me but it, too, is unmarked.

IV It was when Paul Holdway, an engraver at Spode Limited, bought six saucers of this pattern that interest was rekindled in workman's marks on early Spode wares. S.B. Williams illustrates a few of these of page 209 of the third edition of his book, while Arthur Hayden does not mention them and Leonard Whiter considered the study of them 'singularly without profit'. At the time that Whiter wrote his book I would have agreed with him, but not now. On five of the six saucers mentioned were five different marks. By researching these and others a table of marks is being assembled. This subject is discussed later (page 171), but it was this particular pattern and the marks found that showed how important workman's marks can be in providing an additional element of authentication.

Mr Holdway also found four small 'badge coppers'. These are small copper plates with a badge, monogram, or armorial bearings engraved on them. On the back of these particular ones were sections of a Pearl River House engraving: when copper was scarce and expensive, this plate was cut up and re-used.

15. Plate *d.* 20.2 cm. Pearlware. Printed in Cyanine 1 0 5, from a line engraving. Unmarked.

20. Coffee saucer *d.* 12.7 cm. Chinese porcelain. Painted in pale Royal 1 1 0 with gilded edge on cup (not shown) and traces of gold on the rim of the saucer. (1780-95).

16. Dish 38.5cm. *l*. Pearlware. Printed in Royal 1 1 0, Mark I.H. impressed.

17. Dish 47.3cm. *l*. Pearlware. Printed in Cyanine 1 0 5. Unmarked.

SPODE

18. Oval dish 20.3cm. *l*. Pearlware. Printed in blue, with broad gilded line at edge on inner and outer surface (1795-1800).

19. A Malayan Village. The style of construction of the house suggested the name of the pattern previously called Trench Mortar. *Courtesy the Trustees of the British Library*.

21. Coffee cup and saucer. Saucer *d*. 13.4cm. Porcelain. Printed in dark Royal 1 1 0, with gilded edge over a stained dull orange colour. No mark. Attributed New Hall. (1800-1805).

22. Tea cups, saucer and coffee can. Saucer *d*. 12.9cm. Pearlware. Printed in Royal 1 1 0. Cups and saucer are fluted: each has a gilded edge, and shallow ring turned in the base. Attributed to Spode 1795. (The base of the can is slightly translucent).

23. Covered butter dish 13.4cm. *l*. Pearlware. Printed in blue.

26. Tea cup and saucer Saucer *d*. 13.4cm. Porcelain. Printed in Ultramarine
1 0 8, with gilded edge, and foreground painted. No marks. Possibly New Hall (*c*.
(*c*. 1810).

24. (*left*) **Coffee pot** 26.8cm. *h*. Pearlware. Printed in Ultramarine 1 0 8. No marks. Attributed to Spode. (*c*. 1795).

25. (*above*) **Coffee cup, pearlware.**

27. (*below*) **Group of shards**. Pearlware. Printed in flowing Cyanine 1 0 5; parts from a bowl excavated at Fort Cumberland in New Brunswick Canada. *Courtesy Material Culture Research (Archaeology), National Historic Parks and Sites Branch, Parks Canada.*

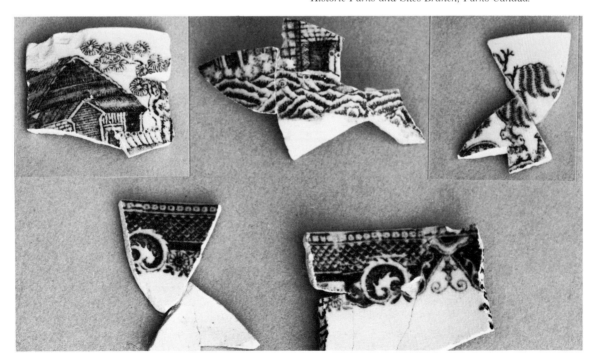

28. Plate *d*. 20.6 cm. Porcelain. Printed in Cyanine 1 0 5, with the colour filling in between the lines to cause an indistinct picture. Mark S printed in blue.

left: plate in grey-blue, right: plate in Midnight with controlled flow, below: coffee can and saucer in Smalts.

hand-painted blues: left: Saxe, right: Arabian.

The selection of blue and white works in the Chinese style by Spode
and other makers shows the range of blue tones possible.

On the left, objects in Cyanine, in the centre, Royal and on the right Ultramarine.

Four of the most common patterns.

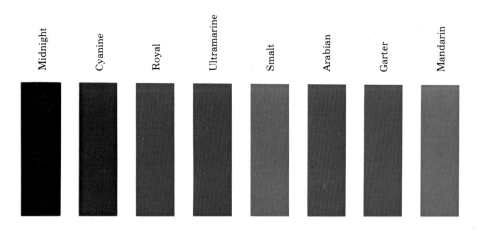

Midnight Cyanine Royal Ultramarine Smalt Arabian Garter Mandarin

Note on the tones of cobalt blues

The idea of indicating the tone of blue on a ceramic item by reference to a system of standard colours was suggested by an article by Cyril Williams-Wood in 1976.[212] Since then the colours of items have been recorded, using the numbering system of the British Standards Institution, *Colours for Specific Purposes. 381C : 1964*. The names used, however, seem inappropriate for identifying old blue and white wares, so the names used by the British Colour Council in the *Dictionary of Colours for Interior Decoration*, 1949 have been adopted.

Name used in this book	British Standard 381C		Approximate Munsell Reference	British Colour Council Number
	No.	Name		
Mandarin	107	Strong blue	2.5 PB 4/10	CC 135
Garter	109	Middle blue	2.5 PB 3/7	CC 136
Arabian	104	Azure blue	5 PB 3/8	CC 143
Smalt	166	French blue	7.5 PB 3.5/12	CC 147
Ultramarine	108	Aircraft blue	7.5 PB 2.5/10	CC 148
Royal	110	Roundel blue	7.5 PB 2.5/8	CC 142
Cyanine	105	Oxford blue	7.5 PB 2/6	CC 150
Midnight	106	Royal blue	7.5 PB 2.5/10	CC 293

Mandarin blue. A descriptive name for one of the blues specially produced for China by British dyers at the beginning of the twentieth century.

Garter blue. The colour used for the ribbon of the Most Noble Order of the Garter.

Arabian blue. A descriptive colour name used for one of the many blue tones originally produced from Indigo and found in Oriental textiles of very early date.

Smalt. The name of a pigment made by pulverising glass coloured by cobalt. This tone exactly matches a sample of smalt in my collection which was given to me by Mr Hunstadbraten of Modum.

Ultramarine. The genuine ultramarine was extracted from Lapis Lazuli, brought from beyond the sea.

Royal blue. A richer and brighter colour than is suggested by BSIC 106, and was once used for smalt.

Cyanine. A name derived from the Greek word *cyanos* – dark blue, and originally used in the paint trade. The colour is slightly more blue than Delft blue (Br. Col. Council CC 144, Munsell reference 5.0 PB 3/2). Alternative names recognised for cyanine are Chinese blue, Oxford blue and Mazarine. I have not used the name Oxford because the BCC colour of that name (CC 288) is darker, while the name Mazarine has latterly been applied to a much lighter tone for use in textiles (BCC /45).

Delft blue. Slightly darker than Cyanine, it is the darkest tone found on Delft pottery.

Ming blue. Slightly brighter than Cyanine, it is typical of the soft-tone, or greyish blue of the ceramics of the earlier period of the Ming dynasty – fourteenth to fifteenth centuries. (BR. Colour Council CC 287, Munsell reference 2.5 PB 3/2.)

Nanking blue. (Br. Colour Council CC 140.) This describes a blue illustrated in Chinese silks.

9 Patterns in the Chinese Idiom

THIS CHAPTER includes a group of Chinese landscape patterns which are all of early date of manufacture, but for which a Chinese prototype is unknown. Until one does appear, it seems prudent not to classify them as reproductions but as patterns in the Chinese idiom. The patterns included here are Bungalow, Buddleia, Temple with Panel, Forest-Landscape, and three unidentified Chinese landscapes. There are three more patterns which are considered to come within this group: Tall Door, Net, and Flying Pennant. The first two may be much earlier than was thought at one time, and this is why they are included here.

Bungalow

Two items only in the Bungalow pattern have been reported. The first is a cream jug on underfired china in the Old Oval shape which is marked S P O D E. A second piece, also in Old Oval shape, is a very fine teapot of bone china which, though not marked S P O D E, has the characteristic mark of the workman. Until a factory name is found for this, it has been called Bungalow pattern, and may date from the very early 1800s (Figs. 1 to 3).

Buddleia

Leonard Whiter called this pattern Temple-Landscape First, but his nomenclature can be confusing, in that he chooses the border as the point of reference rather than the centre, and two different centre patterns can share the same border. It has been suggested that the tree by the bridge might be *Buddleia Lindleyana*, and, on the analogy of Willow Pattern, the name Buddleia Pattern is here adopted. In some ways the pattern resembles Two Temples II, but there are sufficient distinctions, for example, the placing of the bridge, to warrant a separate name, though no Chinese original has yet come to light. Caughley made a similar pattern (Fig. 4) which lacks the tree, and can be compared to a Chinese piece (Fig. 5). The plate illustrated in figure 6 shows the main features of Buddleia Pattern: the bridge with two persons, the one behind carrying a long scroll, the man apparently standing on the shrub in the foreground, and a fence bordering the river's edge. The plate in figure 7, whilst very similar, is included to show how variations occur in patterns probably produced in the same factory: in this instance, the shape and outline of the large central cartouche. Note also the shading to the

1. Cream jug Probably underfired (opaque) bone china. Originally gilded on the edge. SPODE

2. Teapot 16.0cm. *h.* Bone china. Printed in Ultramarine 1 0 8, with gilded edge ornamentation. Mark 47 impressed. (1800-1805) Spode Old Oval shape.

3. Close up of fig. 2 to show details of border.

5. Saucer *d.* 12.5. Chinese porcelain. Painted in Royal 1 1 0.

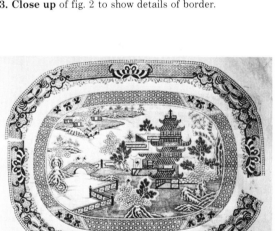

4. Print on cloth Caughley Rag Book, No 112, showing a variation of Buddleia pattern.

left of the left tree which is another of the minor differences.

The vegetable dish base (Fig. 8) was printed originally from a copper plate now in the Spode Museum. Two other versions are illustrated. The plate (Fig. 9) is rather similar to the Spode pattern but the tortured shape of the tree stem and slightly curving shape to the flowers is distinctive and there are no pendants to the roofs of the pagoda on the distant island at top left.

The second plate (Fig. 10) is more similar to the Spode centre design, but the buddleia flowers are fatter, and the border is different, being a trellis

6. Soup plate *d.* 22.6cm. Pearlware. Printed in Royal 1 1 0. Workman's mark in blue. Attributed to Spode. (1795-1805).

design with dagger bead below, and punctuated by eight butterfly motifs. W.L.Little[115] illustrates a plate (his Fig. 75), rather similar to the centre of this one, but with the conventional border, and marked W O L F E impressed. Thomas Wolfe occupied a large factory on the side of the Newcastle branch of the Trent & Mersey canal opposite to Spode's works, and they were partners

7. Deep plate *d.* 23.5cm. Pearlware. Printed in blue.
The main differences to the plate in fig. 6 is in the shape
of the large white area round the central bushes.
Probably Spode. (1795-1805).

9. Plate *d.* 24.7cm. Pearlware. No mark. Note the
tortured shape of the tree.

10. Plate *d.* 23.0cm (approx). Pearlware. Printed in
blue. Unmarked.

11. Soup plate *d.* 22.6cm. Pearlware. Printed in Royal
110. This version, with very little shading, is designated
Forest-Landscape I.

SPODE

8. Deep oval dish 28.2cm. *l.* Pearlware. Printed in blue. Unmarked. The print corresponds exactly to an engraving in the Spode Museum collection.

in coal and china clay enterprises. The border resembles the Turner Buffalo plate border except with a slightly shorter dagger bead.

Forest-Landscape

This seems to be an early pattern by Spode for dinnerware only. The main features of the central scene are the three tall trees in the garden of a splendid house, the man poling a walla walla and what might be a young pine tree in the foreground. The border is the same as that used for Rock pattern, but the nankins are different.

There were two versions. Forest-Landscape I (Fig. 11) may be distinguished by the simpler style of engraving and especially by the lack of shading on the garden surrounding the house. It is this style which suggests that the pattern was a copy of a Chinese one. Forest-Landscape II (Fig. 12) might have been printed from either a newly engraved copper plate, or possibly an old one re-engraved, but the quality is superior even if it lacks some of the charm of the earlier version (Fig. 13).

Temple with Panel

Temple with Panel Pattern was once known on the Spode factory as Temple with Dagger border, or Dagger border and Temple centre, as it is titled in a mid-nineteenth century print record book. Whiter suggests that this might be the pattern described by Simeon Shaw as 'Old Willow with a border of a willow and a dagger', but this descrip-

tion would fit more closely to the Mandarin pattern. Whatever Shaw meant, Whiter's nomenclature Dagger-Landscape is perhaps confusing so this pattern is here called Temple with Panel which identifies the dominant feature of the design.

The temple is austere in appearance with a porch and a panel above it. Set by the water's

12. Plate *d.* 23.7cm. Pearlware. Printed in Royal (darker) 1 1 0. No marks. This later version is Forest-Landscape II.

13. Handled comport on foot, with lid *d*. 27.0cm over handles. Pearlware. Printed in Royal 1 1 0. No marks.

14. Plate *d*. 24.1cm. Chinese porcelain. Painted in Royal 1 1 0.

edge on the left of the scene, an adjoining building is built on stilts over the water. Across to the water to the lower right is a delightful tea house set in a fenced garden; this building in the Spode versions may be compared to the pavilion in the Chinese Buffalo plate (Fig. 14). On the island at the top right are peaked hills, a four-storey pagoda, a skew-bridge and angular rocks. The Spode versions have a trellis-work border and nankin, with a dagger-bead below the border which is shaped to the octagon shape of the flatware.

The Spode wares are very early (1785-95), so the detail of the engraving is somewhat obscured by the flowing of the blue; a print from an engraving (Fig. 15) makes the detail clear. The nearest Chinese piece found is the plate (Fig. 16), but this is more of a mirror image and is not really close enough to be regarded as a prototype. The dish (Fig. 17) is printed from the same engraving as another one which is impressed S P O D E. Similarly, the plate (Fig. 18) is closely similar to a soup plate which is impressed S P O D E.

A version which is very similar to Spode's is shown (Figs. 19 and 20). The three principal differences are that the panel is diamond shaped with no dragon (Spode's is oval with a dragon), and the foreground includes a willow tree of

15. Print on paper from an engraving in the Spode Museum Collection. Temple with Panel pattern.

16. Plate *d*. 23.1 cm. Chinese porcelain. Painted in blue. This is like a mirror image of the pattern produced by Spode.

17. Dish 48.0 cm. *l*. Pearlware. Unmarked. Attributed to Spode. (1785-95).

horizontal spread, while the nankin incorporates four W shape panels.

Versions by other manufacturers include those by Joshua Heath (Fig. 21) and Barker (Fig. 22)[1] Lastly, a variety printed in reverse on flatware (Fig. 23) as well as on holloware (Fig. 24): these two prints are not identical, so they may not be by the same manufacturer.

Unknown Chinese Landscapes

Several of the copper plates for Grasshopper pattern in the Spode storeroom have been engraved on the back of earlier patterns. Two of these patterns are of Chinese landscapes which are unfamiliar. Engraved by fine lines, each is distinctive, but the second pattern (Fig. 25) with its six-storey pagoda, primitive border design and boats is the more unusual. Parts of the design on the

18. Plate *d.* 20.6cm. Pearlware. Printed in dark Royal 110, X mark. Attributed to Spode. (1785-95).

20. Plate *d.* 23.4cm. Pearlware. Printed in dark blue. Note the willow tree added in the foreground.

21. Plate *d.* 24.5cm. Pearlware. Printed in dark blue. Mark I H impressed. (Joshua Heath).

22. Plate *d.* 25.5cm. Pearlware. Printed in Ultramarine 108, mostly line engraved. Mark BARKER impressed. Note the similarity of the trees on the left to those in Long Bridge pattern.

19. Dish 36.4cm. *l.* Pearlware. Printed in blue. X mark in blue. Note the diamond-shaped panel, and the section of non-chinese flowers in the nankin.

24. Sauce boat 16.1cm. *l.* Pearlware. Printed in Cyanine 1 0 5. No mark.

23. Plate *d.* 24cm. Pearlware. Printed in Royal 1 1 0. Temple with Panel pattern in reverse.

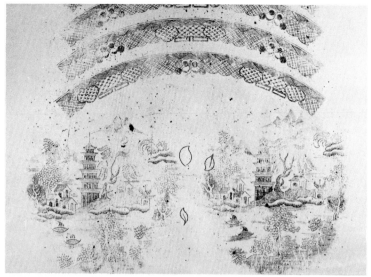

25. Print on paper from another very old engraving with a six-storey pagoda prominent in the centre, and a primitively engraved border.

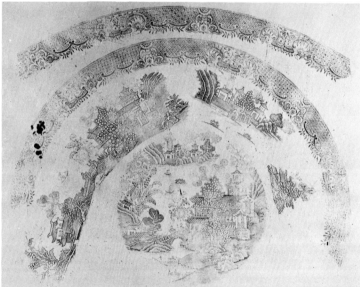

26. Print on paper from a very old engraving in the Spode Limited copper plate stores.

27. Print on paper from a severely treated engraving of a Chinese landscape which is unidentified.

copper plate of the other have been etched (Fig. 26).

Grasshopper pattern was introduced about 1812 when Spode first made stone china. It is not known if these engravings were bought by Spode, but it seems probable. They are illustrated here in case they should have been used by Spode. There seems no reason to doubt that copper was in short supply because of the Napoleonic wars and also that the style of engraving is not that of Spode: the evidence of etching suggests that they were prepared by a trade engraver. The fineness of engraving presents questions of application, for they seem to be cut too shallow for transferring underglaze.

Another Chinese landscape (Fig. 27) has been found on the back of a later engraved design of the Love Chase pattern which dates from the year 1810 to 1815.

Tall Door

The best example of Tall Door is the plate (Fig. 28) which illustrates the somewhat disjointed and imaginative design, suggesting that it might have been derived from a screen or silken textile. An early coffee pot (Fig. 29) and a very finely engraved copper plate in the Spode Museum collection indicate that the pattern is early. A version by another manufacturer (Fig. 30) poses the question about a common source.

28 (*left*) **Plate** *d*. 25.3cm. Pearlware. Printed in Ultramarine 1 0 8. (1810-15). ＳＰＯＤＥ

29. Coffee pot 25.5cm. *h.* Pearlware. Printed in Ultramarine 1 0 8. Workman's mark in blue. Attributed to Spode (*c*. 1800).

30. Saucer *d*. 13.7cm. Pearlware. Printed in dull Ultramarine 108. Unmarked. An unhandled tea cup matches this saucer.

31. Plate *d*. 24.7cm. Pearlware. Printed
in Royal 110. (1805-15). SPODE

33. Vegetable Cover *d*. 19.2cm. across corners.
Pearlware. Printed in Cyanine 105. Panels facing the
knob. Probably Herculaneum.

34. Plate *d*. 24.9cm. Pearlware. Printed
in Ultramarine 108 (1815-20). SPODE

35. Soup plate *d*. 23.9cm. Pearlware.
Printed in blue with brown edge, and
red painted below the rim with
vermicelli design scratched out in white.
(1805-10). SPODE

Net

This intriguing pattern (Fig. 31) takes its name, Net, long-established on the Spode factory, from the central area of hexagonal netting. Four panels, in each of which is a small landscape scene, are set in a background of floral motifs. The border is only found with this pattern which does not include a nankin on plates, but does repeat the border on the Herculaneum dish (Fig. 32). There are many old copper plates of this design on the Spode factory some of which are of the extremely thin sort with very fine engraved lines; so it seems probable that the pattern dates from the 1790s or earlier, although there are numerous examples of later date.

The Herculaneum factory produced this pattern (Fig. 33). Alan Smith[161] has shown that the Herculaneum concern conducted a retail establishment at their Duke Street warehouse in Liverpool in which they sold wares from many other potters, all of those he lists being from North Staffordshire. They include Mason, Minton & Poulson, Ridgway, Rogers and Spode.[II]

It is not known if Spode and Herculaneum had any arrangements concerning the mutual use of this and the Flying Pennant pattern, for the Herculaneum version of the latter differs only slightly from Spode's design.

Flying Pennant

This pattern (Fig. 34) feels as if it is an authentic copy of a Chinese pattern but no original is known. The border, with its meander motifs in dark blue, strikes a strident note reminiscent of the meander, or key, motifs on the border of Willow pattern: it is not found on other patterns. The plate (Fig. 35) has the space between the border and the scroll bead around the centre enamelled in red with vermicelli-like white lines scratched with the sharp end of a wooden stick.

CHAPTER NINE: NOTES

I I am unable to say which Barker this is. Godden lists the three brothers, John, Richard and William Barker potting in Lane End, Staffordshire c. 1800.

II 'Of these manufacturers the one sending the largest amounts of his wares to the Duke Street Warehouse was Josiah Spode, and some idea of the quantities involved may be judged by the following figures of the values of china and earthenware handled by Herculaneum over several years:

1807		£126 19s 7d
1808		£606 7s. 1d.
1809	Purchased	£1,226 10s. 9d.
1810	from	£1,541 6s. 1d.
1811	Josiah	£892 5s. 8d.
1812	Spode	£196·17s. 5d.
1813	by	£286 5s. 1d.
1814	Herculaneum	£65 15s. 3d.
1815		£98 19s. 3d.
1816		£27 7s. 10d.

Just why the trade should have reached its peak in the years 1809-1810 and then fallen almost completely away by 1816 is not fully known, but this might well be accounted for by Spode having found alternative outlets for his wares. It is equally possible that the nationwide recession in trade had its effects also, when manufacturers would prefer to reduce their costs by cutting out commission paid to outside agents.'

32. Dish 58.4cm. *l*. Earthenware. Printed in blue underglaze. Mark HERCULANEUM impressed, (c. 1815). *Photo: The City of Liverpool Museums.*

10 More reproductions of Chinese landscapes

THE THREE PATTERNS included in this chapter were probably made by Spode after 1800 as direct copies of Chinese export porcelain wares. Bridge pattern can be listed with Temple and Broseley as three of the patterns whose names have survived from Spode's time: Willow and Buffalo are two more.

There are three variations of the Bridge pattern produced on the Spode factory. Each of them display the same type of tea house with its circular window, the bridge on the left with two men about to cross, and a border with an unusual drape-like motif. I have seen only the trencher salt in Chinese porcelain (Fig. 1) as an original, but a dish exhibited in Coventry[85] is also illustrated (Fig. 2) as an example of what Spode was trying to reproduce. Examples of Bridge I include toilet wares (Figs. 3 to 5) and drinking vessels (Figs. 6 and 7). Bridge I on pearlware seems to pre-date Bridge II on bone china. The principal difference between the two versions is in the borders, as will be seen.

Bridge II is scarcer and is found on bone china plates and dishes (Figs. 8 and 9). The border is a closer copy of the Chinese examples.

The third version – which has become known as Queen Charlotte (Fig. 10) – is very much later, the pattern 1/3822 being re-engraved in 1884 and called New Bridge. This original factory name is adopted because there is in fact no foundation to the story that it was chosen by the Queen.

While there appear to be but few examples of Bridge pattern on stone china, there are at least two armorial pieces with the border of Bridge II (Figs. 11 and 12). These were obviously made as replacements for Chinese porcelain services. David Howard in *Chinese Armorial Porcelain* illustrates about fifty objects which use the border of Bridge

II and dates the period when this border was popular to 1780-1820, spanning the end of the reign of the Emperor Ch'ien Lung and the beginning of that of Chia Ch'ing.

The principal feature of each of the Bridge borders is the drape which occurs on no other comparable border design. Bridge I border has a rosette in place of the butterflies on Bridge II. Bridge II border has two butterflies, one facing outwards and the other darker one facing inwards, while the drape is shorter. New Bridge border shows distinct differences in the drawing both of the drape and butterflies.

Collectors interested in Chinese export porcelain will have recognised in these patterns three of the most common borders found on blue and white wares. In North America all these borders seem to be known under the general name of Fitzhugh style.

Unfortunately, the name Fitzhugh has been as indiscriminately used for export porcelain styles as the name Willow for Chinese landscape patterns. The name was first used, it appears, by Sir Algernon Tudor-Craig in 1927 when describing armorial service. In the following year, when writing in the *Antiques Magazine* for August,[177] he listed four Fitzhugh style services, and suggested that the name might have been derived from Foochow: 'Last, but not least in interest, we find, about 1800, the Fitzhugh pattern, so called in America only owing to the fact that an old sea captain, trading from Salem, Massachusetts to China, used to buy large consignments of this porcelain at Foochow and return with it to his home port for his wife to sell during his next trip. She, dear lady, apparently did not hold with such outlandish names: so Foochow became Fitzhugh and thus remains to this day.

This porcelain is found either in blue, green or

1. Trencher Salt 8.8cm. *l.* Chinese porcelain. Painted in Cyanine 1 0 5. From a service whose design may have been the model for Spode's Bridge pattern.

2. Dish Chinese porcelain. Painted in blue.

Spode

3. Covered toothbrush box 20.0cm. *l.* Pearlware. Printed in blue. Marks Impressed, on cover, and in blue on base. This design is Bridge I. (1800-1810).

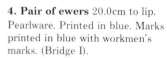

4. Pair of ewers 20.0cm to lip. Pearlware. Printed in blue. Marks printed in blue with workmen's marks. (Bridge I).

5. (*left*) **Bourdalou** 25cm. *l.* overall. Pearlware. Printed in blue. Mark D in blue. (Spode).

6. (*below left*) **Handled pitcher** 17.2cm. *h.* Pearlware. Printed in Ultramarine 108. Attributed to Spode (1805-1810).

7. (*below*) **Handled mug** *d.* 9.9cm. Pearlware. Printed in Royal 110. Probably Spode (1800-1805).

8. Dish 23.9cm. *l.* Bone china. Printed in Ultramarine 1 0 8. This design is Bridge II (1800-10).

9. Plate *d.* 24.1cm. Bone china. Printed in Cyanine 1 0 5. Attributed to Spode (*c.* 1800).

10. Plate *d.* 24.8cm. Stone china. Printed in dark Ultramarine 1 0 8 with gilded edge. Marks impressed, printed in green and in red. Copeland (1906). This design is New Bridge.

rust red, and carries a wide spearhead border in one of these colours. The centre displays four large peonies grouped round a shield, or starlike circle surrounding a crest or other simple design.'

Here Tudor-Craig describes exactly the pattern which David Howard has been forced to call True Fitzhugh. He concludes[93] that the name Fitzhugh must have been used in the nineteenth century, although perhaps not too much credence should

be given to the tale of the captain's wife. Following a series of articles on Chinese Export Porcelain, or Oriental Lowestoft as it was known, which ran in *Antiques Magazine* in 1928 under the editorship of Homer Eaton Keyes, Sydney Thompson, the New York agent for W.T. Copeland and Sons, selected a number of early styles of Chinese export wares which had been popular in America from 1784, and among these was one called Fitz-

11. Plate *d.* 20.8cm. Stone china. Border printed in Royal 1 1 0 with a narrow bead in gold and red below the nankin; brown edge.

Stone China

12. Plate *d.* 20.7cm. Stone China. Border printed in Royal 1 1 0, with a gold, red and green entwined bead below the nankin. Gilded edge and line.

Stone China

hugh. These patterns were engraved at the Spode factory in Stoke-on-Trent to enable the sales of this range to exploit the growing interest in this particular type of porcelain. This range was called Spode's Lowestoft and a small booklet with this title was issued about 1929 to illustrate the pedigree of Spode's reproductions. Two of the patterns, Fitzhugh and Gloucester, had been produced by Spode about 1800 and remain today as popular as ever. This Fitzhugh pattern had the four flower sprays, central medallion and trellis diaper border of True Fitzhugh.

More confusion was introduced in 1935 when Lloyd Hyde in his book *Oriental Lowestoft* applied the name to the border alone presumably because it had a border to the design of four flowers. Recent writers have tried to explain the confusion but only Howard has attempted a solution; while here recognisable names for the borders are recommended, specialists in Chinese export wares may not readily wish to adopt Spode pattern names merely for clarity.

In an attempt to unravel the problem for the future, the following names are suggested:
True Fitzhugh: Four groups of flowers with objects surrounding a medallion-like design, in the centre. The border of trellis diaper with a bead below of daggers, or spearheads, and dumb bells.

Fitzhugh: The same pattern but with the medallion replaced by an armorial device or monogram, etc. Patterns with other border designs should be distinguished correctly, e.g. by using names for the two principal borders which I recommend should be as follows:
Cincinnati border: that familiar in America as used for the George Washington Service and closely copied by Spode as Bridge II. (Butterfly, Honeycomb and Drape – BHD)
Butterfly, Trellis and Key (BTK): as closely copied by Spode as Temple-Landscape II. Most of the plates illustrated in Elinor Gordon's Plate IX have borders of this kind.[76]

Temple-Landscape

The bridge in the foreground with a man carrying an umbrella is the identifying feature of Temple-Landscape patterns. The type of buildings is fairly standard and a sampan plies on the river. There are two types, I and II, which differ in their border decorations, and a variation Parasol which, while different in details, is similar in general design.

Chinese porcelain with this pattern is not uncommon, so it is surprising that only Spode seems to have exploited blue-printed reproductions. John Goldsmith Phillips selected a

13. Plate *d*. 25.0cm. Pearlware. Printed in Royal 1 1 0. Triangular mark in blue. This design is Temple-Landscape, variation Parasol.   *Spode*

14. Plate *d*. 24.7cm. Chinese porcelain. Painted in Cyanine blue. Temple-Landscape I.

platter of this design from the Helena Woolworth McCann collection to illustrate the 'type of porcelain known as Nanking china'. His example is like figure 13 which is here called Temple-Landscape I. He comments that the spear-head (i.e. dagger and dumb bell) border is one of the 'debased version which had entered the vocabulary of the painters of Ching-tê Chên' in the early 1880s. This platter is painted in red-orange colour; the plate in figure 14 is a purply cyanine blue. In the Victoria and Albert Museum is a similar plate, painted in pink, to which the display caption reads 'Painted in the style of English transfer-printed decoration'.

David Howard illustrates[96] a plate from an armorial service for Nesbitt with the same border and nankin as that used on Temple-Landscape II, but with the four groups of flowers of the Fitzhugh pattern; he dates this to the reign of Chia Ch'ing, c.1810. A Spode replacement copied very accurately the original but is characterized by its stiffer decoration. Howard also illustrates[95] examples from armorial services made during the reign of Ch'ien Lung for the families of Hoare and Walcott which use a border and nankin of very similar design to Spode's version Parasol.

The pattern has been known on the Spode factory for many years as Temple and Landscape

and this referred to the version illustrated (Figs. 15 and 16) which is here called Temple-Landscape II, as it seems to be later than variation I. Spode made this first version (Fig. 17) also on stone china like the more common variation II. The border of II is similar to Two Temples I, variation Temple, with the characteristic lozenges in the main panel. These may have been among the later reproductions of Chinese landscapes.

The earlier copies were on earthenware (pearlware), slightly different in detail in the centre, and with dissimilar border and nankin. Whiter called this Parasol Figure, but I think it should be grouped with Temple-Landscape as Variation Parasol (Figs. 13 and 18).

A marvellous Chinese porcelain dish with the same border, and similar nankin, but without the W panels (Fig. 19), confirms the view that the English copied the Chinese.

S.B. Williams shows a dish (3rd. ed. p. 232) which he attributes to Mason, but he gives insufficient information for us to be certain. This is variation I. In the collection of Colonial Williamsburg is a pair of plates, in blue – the one Chinese and the other Mason.

Lastly there is a print in the Caughley rag book which illustrates a design of Temple-Landscape I with the nankin but without the border.

16. (*right*) **Soup plate** *d.* 24.2cm. Stone china. Printed in Ultramarine 1 0 8. (1813-20). This design is Temple-Landscape II.

15. Dish 42.4cm. *l.* Stone china. Printed in Ultramarine 1 0 8. Mark printed in blue. (1833-35).

20. (*right*) **Plate** *d.* 21.3cm. Stone china. Printed in Royal blue, 1 1 0. Mark printed in blue. (*c.* 1833-5).

Spode

18. Dish 47.9cm. *l.* Pearlware. Printed in Royal 1 1 0 (1800-1810). Note the shape of the parasol held by the man on the bridge.

21. (*right*) **Plate** *d.* 24.5cm. Chinese porcelain. Painted in blue with gilded border, lines and edge added in England. (1795-1805). *Courtesy of The Henry Francis du Pont Winterthur Museum.*

19. Dish 35.0cm. *l.* Chinese porcelain. Painted in dark blue. Undoubtedly the original source for Spode's copy. *Courtesy of Kenneth Gill Antiques, Kensington Church St., London.*

17. Plate *d*. 25.2cm. Stone china. Printed in Cyanine 1 0 5 (1813-20). This design is Temple-Landscape I.

Stone China

When Whiter wrote his book on Spode, only an engraved copper plate was known of Lake pattern, which he called Dagger-Landscape, second. On the basis of naming patterns after the central design the name Lake is here chosen.

Since then it seems that all the missing pieces have come to light. First, three sizes of plates were found in 1976. All are on stone china and have been printed from the same copper plate, the smaller sizes losing the outer parts of the scene (Fig. 20). It is almost certain that the engraving was prepared for one customer for replacement plates, and that the design was never used for more than plates.

Secondly, Chinese porcelain plates have been found in the United States, the one illustrated (Fig. 21) having a border of gilding added between the two blue borders, both of which are of continuous trellis diaper. And further Spode plates were found in Canada and England.

Comparing the three plates it will be seen that the Spode copy is an exceedingly accurate one, but that the Copeland and Garrett version introduces the nankin of honeycomb design used for Temple-Landscape variation Parasol, and omits the spearhead bead below the trellis border at the edge.

11   Buffalo Pattern

THE BUFFALO pattern, one of the earliest to be transfer-printed on earthenware was produced by several manufacturers, but it is unusual to find pieces marked with a manufacturer's name, so attribution still remains almost impossible. Details of shape, footrim, glost placing stilt marks, and workman's marks may help, while the visual differences of the borders and centres will provide the principal means of identification.

Several Chinese porcelain examples are known, and undoubtedly the need to match these provided the manufacturers with cause to copy them.[I] With so many potters working in Ching-tê-Cheñn it was inevitable that there should be many variations of a popular design, especially when decoration was entirely by hand. It is not surprising therefore, that there are so many differences in blue printed versions produced in Britain.

The Chinese pieces of Buffalo pattern which are shown here (Figs. 1 to 5) include the following main features:

A tall pavilion on the right with outbuildings, set among trees, and with a rocky cliff on the extreme right.

A man or boy sitting astride a buffalo,[II] which is walking or standing facing to the left, and sometimes held with a cord by the taller of two figures standing in front of a rock on the left side of the scene. Two groups of low rocky outcrops to left and right in the foreground.

An island in the upper centre; one type has a clump of banyan trees, the other has houses with a small pagoda. The nankin or inner border below the shoulder of a plate, is of the honeycomb type, sometimes a single row of cells, sometimes multi-cellular. The border may be as simple as the lozenge-diaper, or as complex as those associated with the landscape designs, which may be called the brocade border.

A comparison of the many pieces seen has suggested a broad division into five main groups, but differences exist between pieces even in the same group, and variations in border designs make attempts at grouping even more complicated. The groups, therefore, are based on the *centre* design only. One can suppose that some of the differences occurred because an engraver was not careful enough when preparing the drawings from which he engraved the copper plates for the different items.[III] Although the purpose of the groups is to facilitate attribution of pieces to one manufacturer or another, it may not always be possible to put a manufacturer's name to a particular piece or group.

At the Spode factory there are seventeen copper engravings of this pattern (Fig. 6) in the museum collection, and seven more have been found in the copper plate safe room. The print record book in the Director's safe notes that thirty engravings were destroyed in 1873, though that figure may include the ones found in the copper plate safe room. These engravings include examples of groups A and B, and actual examples are known on which the transferred prints are identical to some of these engravings. However, Spode's ownership of copper plates does not necessarily mean that Spode engravers produced them nor that every piece of ware of that design was made by the factory. Additional proof has to be found for authentication. The quality and shape of the articles, the standard of blue printing, tell-tale placing marks left after the glost fire, and workman's marks are all indications which guide the collector. Excavations on the Spode factory site from time to time have revealed new evidence, including examples of Buffalo pattern, especially of type B, and such discoveries lend further support to claims of authenticity of manufacture.

1. Coffee cup d. 6.1cm. Chinese porcelain.

2. Saucer d. 11.8cm. Chinese porcelain. Painted in Royal 1 1 0. Note the single cell honeycomb bead.

3. Tea cup d. 7.2cm. Chinese porcelain. Painted, and perhaps from the same service as the handled coffee cup, but painted by a different artist.

4. Soup plate d. 22.3cm. Chinese porcelain. An interesting variation, especially with the brocade border.

5. Teapot 16cm. *h.* Chinese porcelain. Gilded ornamentation.

6. Print on paper from copper plate in Spode Museum.

Attribution therefore can be given only tentatively; many examples are illustrated to show some of the shapes and variations in detail.

The comparative analysis of some of the examples makes it easier to select the group to which a piece belongs.

There are only two or three features by which a Buffalo piece may be clearly placed into a particular group. The most important of these is the top

storey and gable of the pavilion: the way in which the perspective is treated differs in each of the groups, A, B and C, while the detail of the gable end taken with the ridge and finial, also varies between the groups. The shape of the buffalo and drawing of the boy riding it also varies; in particular, the boys in groups B and C have no top knots, but usually do have small ones in group A, and large ones in group D.[IV] The group of the man and the boy in front of rocks on the left of the scene is another feature which may help to place an object into one group, and a brief note on the characteristics of each group follows.

Type A, of which there are several marked S P O D E examples, has a distinct Chinese approach to perspective as seen in the upper floor of the pavilion. The gable of the pavilion is drawn correctly with the apex of the roof exactly below the finial of the ridge. Although this correct drawing occurs in types B and C, the perspective in these differs. In type D, where the perspective is like that in type A, the roof apex is not pointed but is concave in outline. In type E, the roof apex is like that in type D, with an even less accurate representation of perspective, especially in the roof area below the top floor.

The creamware plate (Fig. 7) with its printed mark is relatively late.[107] Another later piece is the pierced basket (Fig. 8). Two pieces of considerable interest are the plate and soup plate (Figs. 9 and 10) of plain, round shape with slightly raised edges to the rim. It was thought that Turner made this shape, but the latter soup plate is marked S P O D E while both were printed from the same engraving. The round dessert dish (Fig. 11), while having a centre almost identical to the Spode pieces, has a nankin in which the rosettes have six petals instead of four: the ridges around the sides may help in identifying the maker when a marked example is found.

Type B, of which there are engravings at the Spode factory, is also competently engraved. The quick reference points are the rounded line on the top floor of the pavilion and the child on the buffalo who appears to have a shaven head. The rosettes in the nankin each have six petals. The shading of the ground below the buffalo is in distinct, horizontal stripes and comparisons can be made with the treatment of this area in the other types.

Several pieces have been printed from copper

Spode

SPODE

8. Handled basket 21.2cm. *l.*
Pearlware. Printed in Royal 1 1 0.
Type A. (1805-1810).

7. Plate *d*. 20.5cm. Creamware. Printed
in Royal 1 1 0. Mark 2 impressed. (1805-
1810). *Spode Museum*.   (SPODE)

9. Plate *d*. 24.5cm. Pearlware. Type A with raised edge
to rim.

engravings at the Spode factory, and workman's
marks are those which are known on marked
Spode examples. Applied to the handles of the
soup tureen (Fig. 12) is a special section of cliff
design, an engraving for which has been found in
the Spode copper plate store. This engraving was
cut for this purpose and is not a narrow piece cut
from the centre pattern: this strip has some
houses half way up the cliff. The shape of this

tureen suggests an early production, and other
examples are known with different Chinese landscape patterns used by Spode. The Argyll (Fig.
13) is another unusual piece of type B, with the
same cliff and house ornamentation on both the
handle and spout. Figures 14 to 16 show other
type B pieces.

The tea cups and saucers, some of which are
gilded, are in a variety of shapes. The tea cup (Fig.

10. Soup plate *d.* 23.2cm. Pearlware. **SPODE** Type A. (1795-1800).

11. Dessert dish *d.* 21.3cm. Pearlware. There are raised radial ridges around the rim, alternately double and single. Gilded edge.

//

15. Dish *d.* 31.8cm. Pearlware. Printed in Cyanine 1 0 5. No marks. Type B.

13. Argyll 18.6cm. *l.* Pearlware. Printed in Royal 1 1 0, Type B. Cliff bead on handle and spout.

.
X

12. Soup tureen and cover 32.0cm. *l.*
Pearlware. Printed in Cyanine 1 0 5.
Identical print to Copper Engraving No. 3.
Type B. Marks 3 impressed on base,   in
blue. Possibly Spode. (*c.* 1790).

SPODE

14. Dish 49.8cm. *l.* Pearlware. Printed in
Ultramarine 1 0 8, employing same engraving
No. 13, and marked 12 impressed (1800-
1805).

16. Dish 51.2cm. *l.* Pearlware. Printed in
Royal 1 1 0. No marks. Type B. Rim with
raised edge.

17) has alternate flutes and ridges on the outer surface, while the inside surface has a circular ridge. This feature has been seen on other pieces and may be a characteristic known to some collectors but so far the name of the manufacturer has not been identified. The elaborately gilded cup and saucer (Fig. 18) is of a regularly fluted and scolloped shape.

An item which was made by several manufacturers is the dessert dish illustrated in figures 19 and 20. This shape is known at Worcester and Caughley as well as at Spode. The Buffalo pattern is of type B, but another, similar dish is of type D.

Late in the Spode period an armorial service was made for the Glover family. Extensive additions were supplied by Copeland & Garrett, of which the covered entree dish illustrated is a good example (Fig. 21).

Type C has a horizontal line within the top floor of the pavilion and the tree growing out of the side of this building has been represented to look more like revolving brushes. The rosette in the nankin often has only five petals and the child riding the buffalo has a shaven head (Figs. 22 to 24).

The characteristics of Type D are numerous. The confused drawing of the gable and top floor have been noted already, while the rider seems too big to be a child and has two distinctive top knots of hair on his or her head (Fig. 25). The rocks have wavy contours rather like those in the unclassified type illustrated by the dish and square salad bowl. The butterfly feature in the border also appears more like a butterfly. The dish (Fig. 26) of type D has rosettes with eight petals. The buffalo is fairly slender with pronounced folding marks on the neck and several double chins. Several examples have printed manufactory marks either of a broken circle or of an eight petalled flower. (It is suggested that this latter mark may have been a piece cut from the bead which sometimes ornaments the back of a handle.)

Type E has a very contented-looking buffalo of more naturalistic shape on which the rider is not so much pointing with his left arm as waving. The butterfly in the border has a sharp saw-tooth feature, while the rosettes are omitted from the nankin. The small soup plate (Fig. 27) is plain and round with a raised edge – reminiscent of the items discussed earlier, but is perhaps not of Spode's manufacture. Another example is illustrated (Fig. 28).

17. Tea cup d. 8.2cm. Pearlware. Ridged inside and fluted. Gilded edge. Type B.

The principal element of this border is the 'circlet of petals' which replaces the 'butterfly' device. This is not the same as that on the Joshua Heath plate, but may stem from a common source, perhaps Caughley. A round plate (Fig. 29) with the scene called Temple (illustrated by Godden),[63] has a border almost identical to that on these Buffalo pieces. (There are differences, however: the Caughley plate has only three rows of petals compared with four on the other pieces: the tiger's tail is solid, and there are other small variations). But against this, the marks are either a circled dot or an eight-pointed floret, or star and there is no published reference to the Caughley production of the Buffalo pattern. A second distinct border which is called 'Lattice panels' is derived from a Chinese original. Spode used this same border when making a replacement (Fig. 30), and an engraved copper plate on the Spode factory suggests he used it also elsewhere (Fig. 31). But the *details* of the border used on marked Spode pieces differ slightly from those of the border used on this variety of Buffalo. Noticeably the open work lattice panel of Spode's is a linking of Y sections, while in borders of non- Spode pieces they are composed of triangles (Figs. 32 and 33). On the square salad bowl (Fig. 34) the engraving of both the scene and the emblems on the outer surface is coarser than on the Spode pieces.

A note on other writers' discussion of this

/ //

18. Tea cup and saucer
d. 12.75cm. Pearlware. Gilded edge,
foot line and gilt decoration added
over blue print. Type B. Marks in
blue on bowl and on saucer, and in
gold S.

19. Dessert dish 24cm. *l.* Pearlware.
Type B. Workman's mark in blue on
inside of foot, which is known as
a *rush* foot.

20. Dessert dish 24.2cm *l.*
Pearlware. Printed in Ultramarine
108. Type B. No marks.

21. Covered entree dish. White earthenware. Buffalo border, into which have been fitted the arms of Glover of Norwich. Copeland & Garrett, (1833-47). *Courtesy Sotheby Parke Bennet & Co. London.*

23. Dish 27.7cm. *l*. Pearlware. Type C. Dark blue print. Three single stilt marks on face as well as three 3-point marks on base. Mark 10 impressed.

26. (*facing page below*) **Dish** 42.4cm. *l*. Pearlware. Printed in Royal 110. Type D. Rosette mark in blue.

24. Dish 42cm. *l*. Pearlware. Printed in Royal 110. Type C. No marks.

22. Plate *d.* 24.8cm. Pearlware. Printed in Royal 110. Type C. Mark F impressed.

25. Plate *d.* 24.8cm. Pearlware. Printed in very dark Royal 110. Type D. No marks.

BUFFALO

Print from engravings of Buffalo pattern . Type B
(by kind permission of Spode Limited)

		A
Pattern type		
Maker		Spo
Object analysed		Plat
1	Pavilion : roof tiling	
2	upper gallery	
3	roof apex	
4	house on left	
5	house on right	
6	steps (?) to right of pavilion	
7	Windows of main buildings	
8	Island, top left, style of banyans	leav show
9	Buffalo : the beast	sler ear
10	the rider	
11	Tall man	Upr
12	Short man	
13	Trees , central group	Sho tre
14	Tree to left of pavilion	
15	Rocks in right foreground	mai are dow
16	Loose stones	tw
17	Rocks behind figures	Som 3 g
	Outer border: butterfly	
	Nankin , inner border: rosette motif	
Profile		
		8 3
Body		Pea
Marks		
Colour		Cyan

This chart shows the principal features of
the five main groups of Buffalo pattern.
There are many variations even within the
same group.

The sketches are not to scale

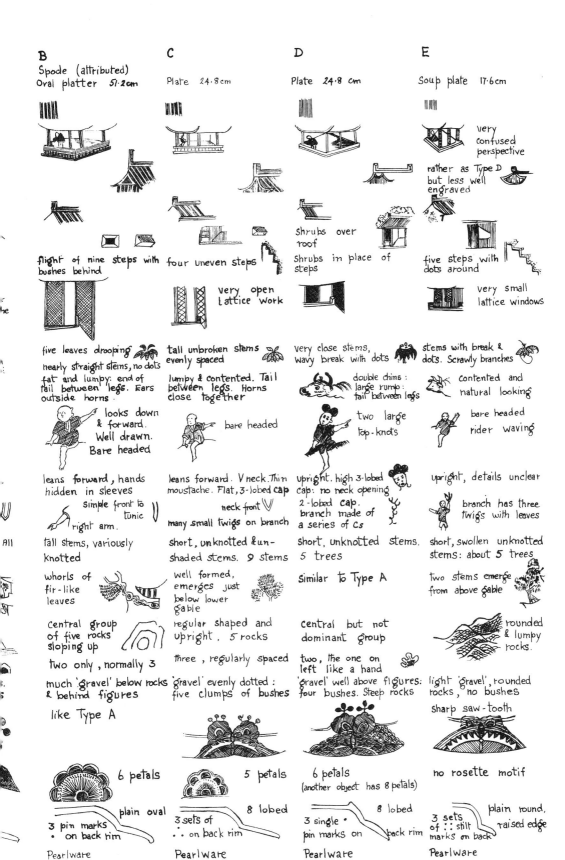

B
Spode (attributed)
Oval platter 51.2cm

C
Plate 24.8cm

D
Plate 24.8 cm

E
Soup plate 17.6cm

very confused perspective

rather as Type D but less well engraved

---

flight of nine steps with bushes behind

four uneven steps

Shrubs over roof
Shrubs in place of steps

five steps with dots around

very open lattice work

very small lattice windows

---

five leaves drooping
nearly straight stems, no dots
fat and lumpy: end of tail between legs. Ears outside horns.

tall unbroken stems, evenly spaced
lumpy & contented. Tail between legs. Horns close together

very close stems, wavy break with dots
double chins: large rump: tail between legs

stems with break & dots. Scrawly branches
contented and natural looking

looks down & forward. Well drawn. Bare headed

bare headed

two large top-knots

bare headed rider waving

leans forward, hands hidden in sleeves
simple front to tunic
right arm.

leans forward. V neck. Thin moustache. Flat, 3-lobed cap
neck front V
many small twigs on branch

upright. high 3-lobed cap: no neck opening
2-lobed cap. branch made of a series of Cs

upright, details unclear
branch has three twigs with leaves

tall stems, variously knotted

short, unknotted & un-shaded stems. 9 stems

short, unknotted stems. 5 trees

short, swollen unknotted stems: about 5 trees

whorls of fir-like leaves

well formed, emerges just below lower gable

Similar to Type A

two stems emerge from above gable

central group of five rocks sloping up

regular shaped and upright. 5 rocks

central but not dominant group

rounded & lumpy rocks.

two only, normally 3

three, regularly spaced

two, the one on left like a hand

much 'gravel' below rocks & behind figures

'gravel' evenly dotted: five clumps of bushes

'gravel' well above figures: four bushes. Steep rocks

light 'gravel', rounded rocks, no bushes

like Type A

sharp saw-tooth

6 petals

5 petals

6 petals
(another object has 8 petals)

no rosette motif

plain oval
3 pin marks
• on back rim

8 lobed
3 sets of
⋮ on back rim

8 lobed
3 single •
pin marks on back rim

plain round,
3 sets of ⋮ stilt raised edge
marks on back

Pearlware
none
Royal 110

Pearlware
F impressed
Royal 110

Pearlware
none
very dark Royal 110

Pearlware
none, except in blue
Cyanine 105

27. Soup plate *d.* 17.5cm. Pearlware. Printed in Cyanine 1 0 5. Type E. Has three groups of four stilt marks beneath the rim, which is raised up at the edge.

28. Plate *d.* 24.2cm. Pearlware. Printed in Royal 1 1 0. Type E. Has three groups of four stilt marks beneath the rim, which has the usual eight scallops and is not raised at the edge. There are 3 single stilt marks on the face of the rim. Probably Wolfe.

29. Plate *d.* 20.8cm. Porcelain. Printed in dark blue with the Caughley Temple pattern, with gilded edge and line below the border. Note only three rows of petals. No mark.

30. Plate *d.* 22.0 cm. Bone china. Printed in bright Ultramarine 1 0 8, with painted additions. Probably intended as a matching. Rock II. 1800-1810.

32. Plate *d.* 23.1 cm. Pearlware. Type B centre, but with Lattice Panels border and false Y-diaper work.

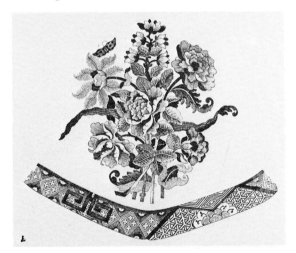

31. Print on paper from Spode engraving for a version of Group pattern. *c.* 1800.

34. Square salad bowl 25.7 cm. *l.* Pearlware. Printed in Cyanine 1 0 5. No mark. There are Fitzhugh-type sprays on the outside.

33. Dish 46.8cm. *l.* Pearlware. Printed in dark blue. Partial rosette mark.

SPODE   ///

35. Supper section 34.2cm. *l.* Pearlware. Type B. (1795-1800).

pattern will be found in the Appendix.

Several writers have included pictures of Buffalo pattern in their works, so I review these to help the reader assess the information on Buffalo pattern that has been published to date. Coysh I illustrates a plate (Fig. 2) of type D, with what he describes as a small six-pointed star mark. He states that the Buffalo pattern was used by several potters in the 1780s and 1790s including Thomas Wolfe

(citing reference to G. Woolliscroft Rhead, *British Pottery Marks* (1910) page 291), Josiah Spode (Williams, Fig. 96) and Joshua Heath (Little, plates 31 and 32). W.L. Little, in the caption to his plate 31, includes Leeds as a manufacturer of this pattern. The plate he illustrates has a centre design of type A, but the border is quite distinct from any that I have analysed, having a circlet of petals in place of the butterfly device. This piece has an impressed mark, and he attributes its manufacture to J. Heath of Hanley (c. 1790).

Another piece impressed I H has the centre and nankin printed from the same engraving as the former plate but with the conventional border. The sauce boat which Little illustrates (plate 32) has the standard nankin and is of type A, but the mark I.H. is raised, not impressed. This can be explained as follows: a piece of flatware, after it has been formed on the plaster of Paris mould, will not be deformed by impressing a marker into the clay because of the support of the mould. A piece of holloware when removed from the mould might be deformed or a strain caused by impressing a marker. The mouldmaker, therefore, carved the mark into the plaster mould, so the clay piece will have the mark raised.

The supper set section (Fig. 35), illustrated by S.B. Williams, is of type B, and has the impressed mark SPODE (p. 127). A shard (Fig. 36) of this group B was excavated on the Spode Works in 1936, being found below the foundations of one of the bottle ovens used for earthenware glost firing: it is thought that these ovens would have been built 1795-1800. Lastly, Whiter (p. 153) illustrates the plate in the Spode Museum collection which is type A.

Bevis Hillier illustrates[89] a plate 'transfer printed in blue with a version of the Willow pattern containing an elephant with a twisted trunk', with TURNER impressed mark (plate 24a) (Fig. 37). This design is one of those enchanting mixtures in which the Staffordshire potters specialised and it must have created much amusement among the table guests. It is not a willow pattern, but the dominant feature is the group of large buildings derived from the Buffalo pattern. Copper No. 14 in the Spode Museum has an elephant with a castle on its back, in place of the buffalo, but is unlike the Turner design in other respects. A bowl (Fig. 38) with this design has the border of figure 31 on the inside and a coarsely engraved floral centre; this centre and border correspond to print records from the Knottingley factory at Ferrybridge.[113]

Another engraved copper (no. 10) is a variation on type B. Probably intended for a tall, slender article, it has no pavilion, cliff or central group of trees: just the central characters, foreground rocks and banyans. What is different is that all the people have feathers in their heads, and the small

36. Shard possibly of soup plate. Pearlware. Excavated on the Spode works below glost oven, 1936.   ///

37. Plate d. 24.4cm. Pearlware. Engraved with line work and printed in a grey blue. Impressed mark TURNER 4 (1790-1800).

38. Bowl *d.* 18.6cm. Pearlware. Printed in Cyanine 105. Unmarked. Attributed to Knottingley factory, Ferrybridge (*c.* 1800).

39. Oval comport 32.9cm. *l.* Pearlware. Printed in Royal 110. Type B with unlocated version of the Feather Heads design. Unmarked.

boy holds three feathers instead of a branch. I call this the Feather Heads, type B. Two vases with this centre are known. A most interesting piece is an oval comport on foot having the centre of type B, and Feather Heads on the outside. The engraving for the centre is in the Spode Museum (Fig. 39), but that for this Feather Heads group has not been located yet. It is almost the same as copper no. 10 but the feathers are not identical. A large handled mug of type C shows a thin feather on the head of the rider only.

CHAPTER ELEVEN: NOTES

I The Buffalo pattern discussed in this chapter must not be confused with that made by the Castleford Pottery (illus. Coysh II, pp 18/19) and appropriately named Buffalo and Ruins Pattern.

II It has been suggested that the rider represents the philosopher Lao-Tzu. He was the author of a book *Tao-Teh-King* which outlines his teaching which is the basis of the religion of Taoism. Lao-Tzu was born in 604 BC and became the keeper of the Royal Library at the court of Chow in the province of Honau. In 517 BC he had an interview with Confucius and in his old age, when the dynasty had grown weak, he set off for the 'regions beyond' on a water buffalo. He became known as 'the Venerable Philosopher' and taught compassion and humility.

III Jewitt[107] says that Minton engraved for Spode, one of his chief employers, a teaware pattern called the Buffalo which continued to be in demand for many years. Is it not likely that he engraved versions for other employers?

IV It is probable that these protuberances are hair. C.A.S. Williams writes 'It is customary to shave the heads of young children, leaving a tuft above one, or each, ear in the case of girls, and one on the top of the head in the case of boys'. It is possible that the rider could be a girl.

12 Long Bridge Pattern

1. Plate *d.* 23.4cm. Pearlware. Printed in Royal 1 1 0.
Mark D.D. & Co CASTLEFORD POTTERY
impressed.

GRESHAM COPELAND, the father of the author, became interested in this pattern when he noticed that on a plate made by Dunderdale (Fig. 1) certain features of the design were similar to those in Forest-Landscape pattern (Fig. 11, Ch. 9), in particular, the young pine tree and walla walla in the foreground as well as two of the tall trees on the right. He collected two other examples of similar plates, one marked LEEDS POTTERY (Fig. 2) and the other SWANSEA (Fig. 3).

The main feature of the pattern is the long bridge, of three even-sized arches, and a junk in the foreground. A temple with wall panels occupies the right centre with a doorway close to the bridge which leads to a tall pavilion on the left of the scene. Two persons, usually bent forward, are crossing the bridge going towards the pavilion. The border usually includes two manuscript scrolls in its design but no insects or butterflies; the nankin is honeycomb with reserve panels in which a floret is set between solid, double fleur-de-lys style motifs.

Godden, in *British Pottery*,[71] illustrated a splendid supper set on a tray (Fig. 4); the shapes of the items were unusual, especially that of the long sections around the outside, each of which in addition has the willow tree. Morton Nance illustrates many pieces of this pattern which is mis-named Swansea Willow Pattern. His examples may be grouped into three sorts: borders with butterfly and no scrolls, the nankin similar to the true Willow pattern; borders with no butterflies but with scrolls, the nankin being of honeycomb cells with reserve panels; one jug which has a willow tree growing immediately behind the temple and overhanging the long bridge. A similar shaped section (Fig. 5) with an impressed SPODE mark is decorated with the true Willow II, and caused some collectors to wonder if Spode had produced this Long Bridge pattern. A more regular shape of supper section (Fig. 6), when compared to a marked Spode one fitted exactly and served to strengthen this theory. Lastly, a soup tureen is known (Figs. 7 and 8) whose shape is the same as two others believed to be Spode, one with Buffalo pattern and another with Buddleia. All these objects have workman's marks corresponding to ones known on Spode wares. There is no other evidence known to show that this pattern was made on the Spode factory, but I would not be surprised if later proof shows that the objects in figures 7 to 10 were indeed by Spode.

Many other examples are included for comparison. The plates (Figs. 11 to 13) for example, have nankins of the radiating circle design instead of honeycomb cells. It is hoped that some attributions may be possible in due course. The plate in figure 14 is identical to shards excavated on the site of the Keeling factory in Hanley during September 1972.[166] This plate is similar to that illustrated in figure 11, but while there is no man in the garden on either plate, in the Keeling design there are no rocks and no man in the doorway.

2. Plate *d*. 24.8cm. Pearlware. Printed in Royal 1 1 0.
Marks LEEDS POTTERY impressed.

3. Plate *d*. 24.5cm. Pearlware. Printed in Royal 1 1 0,
with dull yellow (old gold) edge. Mark SWANSEA
impressed.

6. Supper quadrant section 31.3cm. *l*. Pearlware. Mark in blue. This fits
exactly similar Spode supper sections.

4. Supper set on tray *d.* 69.8cm.
Pearlware. Printed in blue.
Unmarked. The central covered
piece contains a pierced stand for
eggs. *Courtesy of Geoffrey Godden
– Chinaman.*

9. Dish 36.9cm. *l.* Pearlware.
Printed in blue. No mark. Possibly
by Spode.

SPODE

5. Supper set section 36.3cm. overall. Pearlware. Printed in blue. (1795-1800).

7 & 8. Soup tureen and cover. 34.5cm. over handles. Possibly by Spode.

10. Plate *d.* 19.9cm. Pearlware. Printed in Royal 1 1 0. Possibly by Spode.

11. Pierced edge plate *d.* 20.8cm. Pearlware. Printed in blue. No mark. Note six strands of wicker and sharply cut edge.

12. Deep soup plate *d.* 24.9cm. Pearlware. Printed in bright blue. No mark.

13. Plate *d.* 24.1cm. Pearlware. Printed in Royal 1 1 0. Possibly by Keeling (*c.* 1800).

LONG BRIDGE

Pattern	Type A illustra
Maker	
Object analysed	Plate 19.9 cm

Photograph of a plate of Type A

A selection only is included in this chart of the many examples of this pattern.

The Type letters are for distinguishing each variation and have been applied as each analysis was prepared by the author.

The sketches are not to scale

Main building
1 Pinnacle
2 Roof
3 Balcony

4 Gable end

5 Wall panels
6 Doorway & figure

Long bridge
7 Figures
8 Parapet
Pavilion
9 Pinnacle
10 Balcony
11 Panels
12 Tree

13 Junk
note central rope extends to gunwale

Garden
14 Rocks

15 Figure (by wall) stands on open path

16 water's edge

17 Trees

18 Two small junks

Island
19 Two main buildings
20 Trees

Nankin

Profile
8 lok
3 pin marks
• on back rim

Body	Pearlware
Marks	in blue
Colour	Ultramarine 108

B

Type E

Plate 23.9 cm

Type F
Leeds
Plate 24.9 cm

Type G
Swansea
Plate 24.6 cm

Type H
Plate 24.1 cm

24.9 cm

re in door

panels as
Type H but
coarser

panels as
Type B

no
figures
in balcony

panels
tall & thin

no
yardarm

on open
near rocks

stands on
shaded area

as Type A

no figure in garden

both similar to
those in Type A

honeycomb
as Type A

semi-octagon
8 lobed

below rim

8 lobed

3 single
pin marks

8 lobed

semi-octagon
8 lobed

3 stilt
marks below rim

8 lobed

ware

110

Pearlware
none
Arabian 104

Pearlware
LEEDS·POTTERY impressed
Royal 110

Pearlware
SWANSEA impressed
Royal 110

Pearlware
— in blue
Royal 110

14. Plate *d*. 18.5cm. Pearlware. Printed in pale Royal 1 1 0. Similar to shard excavated on site of Keeling factory in Hanley. Attributed to James Keeling (1795-1805).

2. Plate *d*. 25.1cm. Stone china. Painted in saxe blue (grey-blue) with excellent freedom in imitation of the style of the original. Mark impressed.

SPODES
NEW·STONE

1. Dish 37.2cm. *l*. Stone china. Painted in bright Ultramarine 1 0 8. The dish has a combed base. Mark 47 printed in blue.

Stone China

SPODE WAS ABLE and willing to produce special items to match a customer's Chinese piece or to supply an item which, although not a replacement, was one to enhance the completeness of the service. Generally these *matchings*, as they are called in the trade, were painted on stone china and therefore must date after 1812.

The finest of these is a dish in the style of Two Temples II (Figure 1), but with many variations. (Illustrated by Whiter, Plate 1.) A quite charming plate (Figure 2) has all the spontaneity of the Chinese artist so that it was almost passed over by the collector as Chinese. The two coffee cups (Figure 3) illustrate how Spode seems to have been willing even to make an item in clay so that his replacement might match closely its Chinese prototype. Another sauce boat stand is shown (Fig.4).

Three octagonal plates, one (Figure 5), strictly octagonal, painted so finely as to look almost like a print, the second (Figure 6) painted with bolder strokes in a deft style; the third painted to simulate the Chinese artist's style. (Fig.7)

With this group of *matchings* are several which have borders printed in blue, but the centres are painted in enamel colours. A plate with a border unlike any other I have seen is illustrated (Fig. 8); the centre is well painted and might be mistaken for a Chinese piece if not examined closely. A soup plate, (Figure 9) uses the Grasshopper border and what appears to be a painted blue outline to the centre which has been enamelled over the glaze. This pattern is sometimes seen on Chinese porcelain (Fig.10) and, more rarely on delft.

An important service, known to me as the Pitts-Tucker service (Figure 11), has a history which was recorded in correspondence between my father and a spinster descendant of the family, Amy B. Pitts-Tucker. Her father (b. 1831, d. 1919) told her that the Chinese pieces were paid as barter by the sea captains who, docking at Appledore and Bideford Quay, came to her grandfather who was a lawyer there. Because the Chinese pieces acquired in this way were insufficient, he had them copied by Spode to complete the service.

Other patterns with painting

Two other patterns with blue printed outlines are included here. The Chinese panel pattern (Figure 12) in a rather simple style occurs on bone china and pearlware, the outline filled in with pink enamel on the glaze. Apart from a number of pieces which I have seen, copper plates for use on dishes are on the Spode factory. The other pattern, Spode's Landscape is copied from Chinese prototypes. (Figure 13) The blue printed design is enamelled, gilded on glaze, and continued in production on a variety of bodies up until 1939.

A plate of this pattern made in 1912 is a good example of Flow blue (Fig. 14). On the reverse is the inscription, etched into the glaze:

Standard Colour
For Canton all must match
this Plate
Not to be taken from Printers Square

(Unfortunately the hazy 'aura' to the print which is the characteristic of flow blue has not reproduced in the photograph.)

SPODE.

3. Left Coffee cup 6cm. *h.* Chinese porcelain. Painted in Cyanine 1 0 5, with gilded edge, bead below blue border inside and gilded foot line. **Right** Coffee cup 6cm. *h.* Stone china. Painted in Royal 1 1 0, with identical gold treatment. Mark painted in red.

SPODES NEW·STONE

4. (*left*) **Stand** 18.1cm. *l.* Stone china. Painted in Arabian 1 0 4.

SPODES NEW·STONE

5. (*left below*) **Octagon plate** *d.* 21.3cm across flats. Stone china. Painted in blue to match a chinese piece. Mark impressed.

SPODES NEW·STONE

6. (*below*) **Octagon plate** *d.* 22.8cm. across flats. Stone china. Painted in Royal 1 1 0, to match a Chinese piece, perhaps made for the Dutch market. Mark impressed.

7. Plate *d*. 21.9cm. Stone china. Painted in Royal 1 1 0, with brown enamel edge. The foot rim is yellowish as in chinese examples.

8. Plate *d*. 25.4cm. Stone china. Border printed in pale Ultramarine 1 0 8 from very fine engraving with old gold edge. Centre painted on glaze in enamel colours.

9. Soup plate *d*. 23.0cm. Stone China. Border printed in Cyanine 1 0 5. Between the border and edge, a painted red band with *joo-i* panels in blue, and link bead gilded over the red. The centre outline painted in blue and enamelled on glaze. Gilded edge. (Pattern 2372) *Courtesy Spode Museum.*

10. Plate *d*. 22.9cm. Chinese porcelain. Painted in blue (*c*. 1755) *Courtesy Christopher Sykes Antiques.*

11. Group of items of dinnerware. Left, soup plate *d.* 22.2cm. Chinese porcelain. Border painted in Cyanine 105, with painted centre. Middle, covered vegetable dish, and right, plate *d.* 24.5cm. Stone china. Border printed in Cyanine 105, with painted centre. Mark printed in blue (1820-25). From the Pitts-Tucker service.

12. Plate *d.* 24.8cm. Bone china. Printed outline in Ultramarine and filled in with pink on glaze; veins of leaves gilded. Marks printed in blue and in red.

13. Plate *d.* 21.6cm. Chinese porcelain. Painted in Cyanine 105, centre painted in colours. (1780-1800).

SPODE

14. Plate *d.* 27.0cm. White earthenware. Printed in Midnight 106 and showing flow properties. Marks impressed.

THE ORIGINAL meaning of the word trophies was a collection of the arms of a beaten enemy. The swords, spears, arrows, battle axes and shields were hung on a wall surmounted by a helmet. Later, the meaning was extended to include arrangements of objects related to a particular pursuit such as music, hunting or games.

In Chinese symbolism, similar arrangements of objects have been known as Hundred Antiques, although the word hundred should be interpreted as meaning sundry or various. These objects comprise the Eight Treasures and the Four Treasures. The Eight Treasures include four distinct arrangements: firstly, the Eight Ordinary Symbols – the Pearl, Lozenge, Stone Chime, Rhinoceros' Horns, Coin, Mirror, Book and Leaf. Another group are the Eight Precious Organs of Buddha's body. The Eight Auspicious Signs are the Wheel of the Law, Conch-shell, Umbrella, Canopy, Lotus, Jar, Fish and Mystic Knot. The final group comprise the emblems of the Eight Immortals of Taoism – Sword, Fan, Flower-basket, Lotus, Flute, Gourd, Castanets and Musical Tube, or drum.

The Four Treasures are represented by the symbols of the four fine arts: music, chess, calligraphy and painting. The Hundred Antiques might include any of these together with conventional representations of sacrificial vessels, flowers and animals.

Designs on ceramics frequently include four separate groupings of these trophies, and Spode produced several patterns using these groupings with different borders. Examples of three of these are known, while a fourth is recorded in the print record book of 1864. This book records a print of each design with the name of the border and that of the centre, thus, Etruscan Border and Trophy centre. Whiter used these names but contracted them thus, Trophies-Etruscan, and that nomenclature is here followed.

The four patterns recorded are: Nankeen Border and Trophy centre (Trophies-Nankin), Etruscan Border and Trophy centre (Trophies-Etruscan), Marble, or Mosaic, Border and Trophy Centre (Trophies-Marble), and Dagger Border and Trophy Centre (Trophies-Dagger).

Trophies-Nankin is the earliest of the Trophies patterns: it might have been produced before 1800 (Fig. 1). The border is the same as that used for Willow pattern, and it is interesting that the Spode factory knew this by the name Nankeen or Nankin. The design of the 'hundred antiques' captures the Chinese feeling (Fig. 2).

Trophies-Etruscan is a later pattern completely re-engraved; an enamelled version is first recorded as Number 4155, corroborating Jewitt's dating of 1825 (Fig. 3). An underglaze version is Pattern B110.

Trophies-Marble is only known on the gadroon shape with the blossoms tinted underglaze in orange (Fig. 4). The Hundred Antiques centres use the same engravings as Trophies-Etruscan. The pattern is number B111, and on the page is written 'Engravings destroyed – re engraved about 1896'.

For Trophies-Dagger, only a print in the record book is known (Fig. 5). Unhappily another print at the end of the same book is given the same title but the print is of True Fitzhugh. It may be that Leonard Whiter knew of this book which may have suggested to him that Dagger Border and Trophy centre was the 'authentic' name for Fitzhugh.

It will be seen from illustrations of the True Fitzhugh pattern (see fig. 6) that the group around the centre are neither Trophies nor Hun-

1. Plate *d.* 23.1cm. Pearlware. Printed in blue, slightly flowed. Spode (1800-1805). This is the Trophies Nankin pattern.

SPODE /

3. Plate *d.* 24.9cm. Pearlware. Printed in Ultramarine 108. This is the Trophies-Etruscan pattern.

SPODE
SPODE

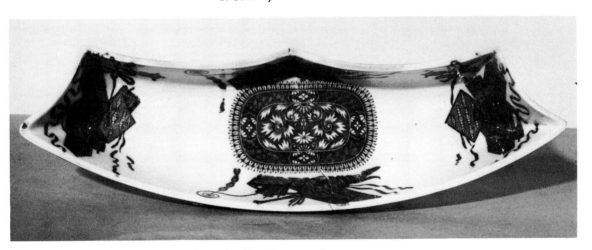

2. Supper set section 32.3cm overall. Printed in blue. (1800-1805). SPODE

dred Antiques. They are arrangements of flowers dominated by either a peony or a chrysanthemum with objects representing the Chinese Four Treasures.

The Flowers of the Four Seasons are peony, lotus, chrysanthemum and prunus. The Peony for Spring is also a symbol of riches, honour, love affection and feminine beauty. The Lotus for Summer, because of its numerous seeds, is a symbol of fruitfulness. The flower also represents purity and perfection. The Chrysanthemum for Autumn is a symbol of steadfast friendship associated with a life of ease and retirement. The Prunus for Winter is a symbol of life itself.

Associated with these in the Fitzhugh groups are symbols representing the Four Treasures, or Accomplishments. These are shown as music, by an embroidered lyre-case, or musical instrument,

4. Plate *d.* 23.5cm. Pearlware. Printed in Ultramarine 1 0 8, with the flowers coloured in with orange, underglaze.

5. Print in Print record book, commenced 1864. Dagger Border & Trophy Centre. *Courtesy Spode Museum.*

6. Close up views of the four motifs which occur on the true Fitzhugh pattern.

7. Dish 53.1cm. *l.* Chinese porcelain. Painted in Royal 1 1 0.

chess, by a chequers board, calligraphy, by a pair of books, and painting, by a pair of scrolls.

The central design incorporates dragons, regarded as lords of the heavens and the seas. The dragon is the genius of strength, goodness and life itself. They surround a motif which has the appearance of an open pomegranate; the pomegranate is a Buddhist sign and, owing to the numerous seeds of the fruit, is an emblem of posterity.

We have already discussed the conclusions of David Sanctuary Howard regarding the use of the name Fitzhugh to describe the Bridge II and Temple-Landscape II borders. The origin of the name itself has been traced to the FitzHugh family who still possess a few examples of the porcelain service. J.B. Sander Holmes writing in the American magazine *Antiques*[91] explained that members of the FitzHugh family had held important positions in the service of the East India Company at Canton. First, Captain William FitzHugh sailed his ship to the Orient in 1703 reaching Chusan in 1704,although there is no record of him going on to Canton. He had three sons, one of whom, Thomas, born in 1728, was employed by the East India Company as 'writer' (or junior clerk) to the supercargo on the ship *Sandwich* bound for Canton in 1746. He visited Canton on several more occasions and was President of the Select Committee there between 1779 and 1781, becoming a director of the Company in 1786. His son, also Thomas, was at Canton until later in the 1790s. Captain Williams's nephew, William, was a supercargo from 1775 to 1791, and the records show that he spelt his name Fitzhugh, without the capital H. It is possible that the younger Thomas FitzHugh brought back a porcelain service, without armorial decoration, to his home near Wrexham in Wales in about 1786, or alternatively his father brought one back in 1781 when he returned from China.[92]

It does seem clear, however, that this pattern only (Fig. 7) should rightly be called True Fitzhugh. An earlier and somewhat coarser Chinese style of the same pattern had been available in Canton about 1765-70, and it was probably from this that the very finely executed service for the FitzHugh family was developed. Spode was probably making the pattern as early as 1808 or even before that, possibly as replacements for the Fitz-Hugh family at Wrexham, only about thirty-five miles from Stoke-on-Trent.

The soup plate (Fig. 8, right) has the appearance of having been made before 1800, whilst the soup plate of octagonal shape (Fig. 9) accords with an 1808 date: the octagonal shape is in imitation of a Chinese original. This has a simpler form of dagger border which omits the dumb bells between the dagger or spear heads. The earliest example of stone china known are those made in the first few years of the Copeland & Garrett partnership (Figs. 10 and 11). The latter is of the style V12 in Howard's classification of Chinese armorial porcelains; this, a blue trellis diaper border with spearhead bead below and the arms with supporters, is of the Ch'ien Lung period, about 1790. Swansea also made a coarser form of the pattern, and the two items in figures 12 and 13 are probably from that factory, although more finely engraved than the examples illustrated by Morton Nance. Another fine reproduction is illustrated (Fig. 14).

9. Soup plate *d.* 21.7cm. (across flat sides). Pearlware. Printed in Ultramarine 108 (*c.* 1808).

SPODE

8. Comparison *Left*, plate *d.* 24.0cm. Chinese porcelain. Painted in blue. *Right*, soup plate *d.* 24.1cm. Pearlware. Printed in deep Royal 110. Probably Spode (1795-1800).

10. Plate *d.* 23.4cm. (across flat sides). Stone china. Printed in Ultramarine 108. Copeland & Garrett (1833-37).

11. Plate *d.* 23.5cm. (across flat sides). Stone China. Printed in dark Ultramarine 108. In the centre the coat of arms of the Corporation of the City of London. Copeland & Garrett (1833-37).

12. Plate *d*. 25.2 cm. Pearlware. Printed in Royal 1 1 0. Rosette mark in blue.

14. Plate *d*. 24.0 cm. Pearlware. Printed in Ultramarine 1 0 8 beneath a clear glaze. No mark.

13. Dessert dish 25.3 cm. *l*. Pearlware. Printed in Royal 1 1 0. Rosette mark in blue.

THERE ARE twelve patterns in this group for which Chinese prototypes are known. These are Fence, Spotted Deer, Lattice Scroll, Marble, Bowpot, Bude, Grasshopper, Lange Lijzen, India, Dragons, Group, and Chinese Flowers.

Fence

As to Fence, S.B. Williams illustrates a Spode plate (Fig. 1) compared to a Chinese plate with a similar type of design (Fig. 2); these are illustrated here. Williams states that no two pieces of the Chinese portion of the service were alike, although the borders and inner double-scroll bead were similar; it is not surprising that Spode's reproduction is different. The clarity of the print of the plate in this example suggests that it is a late example and possibly was printed from several engravings to help match the particular Chinese service. The two other illustrations (Figs. 3 and 4) show objects printed in a much softer greyish flowing blue with a narrow cell bead and no full border. They seem to be of early date: about 1800 to 1805. Whiter draws attention to the use of the floral sprays from the border of Group pattern on Williams' plate, and this would indeed date it to about 1810-12.

Spotted Deer

The illustration (Fig. 5) shows a print from an engraving in the Spode Museum, though such a Spode piece is unknown. Another Staffordshire manufacturer produced it in the mid-nineteenth century.

Lattice Scroll

Two Chinese plates with this design (Fig. 6) are known and it was popular at one time, if the number of old Spode engravings are any guide. Whiter dates the pattern to c. 1810 when enamelled versions, numbers 1680-1684 were recorded. In the late nineteenth century the pattern name was Vermont (Figs. 7, 8 and 9).

Marble

This name occurs in the 1864 Print Record Book, although Mosaic and Cracked Ice and Prunus have been used in the past – none is quite accurate. The design clearly derives from a Chinese prototype similar to that illustrated in figure 10. Traditionally, it seems this pattern represents the early spring when the ice on the ponds begins to crack and the prunus blossom falls upon it. Whiter has traced the earliest reference to pattern number 3667 introduced in about 1821. The sheet was used in conjunction with other patterns notably Tumble-down Dick, pattern number 3716. Figures 11 to 14 show examples.

Bowpot

This pattern can be dated to about 1812, when, as pattern numbers 1867-9 show, it was enamelled. Figures 15 to 17 show examples of this continuously popular design, and figure 18 a Chinese model for it. A bone china plate with the pattern number N244 has the characteristics of Spode's manufacture being of the right type of body, etc., and the Bowpot design printed in fine black lines and enamelled in green. This number, along with many other early ones is missing from the Spode pattern book. It is noteworthy that the numbers which are included are prefixed with N^O (see Whiter plate 106): this continues up to N^O 353, and are mostly border patterns normally associated with cream coloured earthenware. If this plate is by Spode it could be dated 1802.

Bude

This pattern is only known on stone china with gilded leaves and ornamentation (Fig. 19) as number 2219, c. 1814. But the Chinese plate (Fig. 20) is also gilded so Spode seems to have been consistent in reproducing on stone china the expensive designs with gold and enamels.

1. Plate *d.* 25cm. Body unknown. Mark uncertain (Spode) Fence pattern.

2. Plate Chinese porcelain.

3. Tea cup and saucer Bute shape; saucer *d.* 13.3cm. Pearlware. Printed in blue with gilded edge and stroke down cup handles. Attributed to Spode.

5. Print on paper from engraving in the Spode Museum of the Spotted Deer pattern.

6. Plate *d*. 20.0cm. Chinese porcelain. Painted in Cyanine 1 0 5.

11. Plate *d*. 21.5cm. Pearlware. Printed in Ultramarine 1 0 8. Marble pattern. (1821-30).

9. Plate *d*. 21.0cm. Pearlware. Printed in Ultramarine 1 0 8. Lattice Scroll pattern (*c*. 1810).   Spode   *

SPODE

4. Supper set section 32.0cm. *l.*
Pearlware. Printed in blue. (1800-
1805). Fence pattern.

SPODE

7. Custard cups on stand
d. 24.6cm. Pearlware. Printed in
Royal 1 1 0. Mark 36 in blue. A
seventh cup rests on a raised central
plinth. *Courtesy Spode Museum.*

SPODE

8. Dish 41.5cm. *l.* Pearlware.
Printed in Royal 1 1 0. Unidentified
coat of arms in the centre.
(1810-15).

10. Covered dish *d.* 17.7cm.
Chinese porcelain: there are five
compartments in the base. A
similar design may have provided
the prototype for Marble pattern.
Courtesy Spode Museum.

SPODE

12. Oval dessert dish 26.5cm.
l. and cream jug 10cm. *h.* Printed
in blue.

SPODE

14. Coffee cup and saucer *d.*
14.0cm. Pearlware. Printed in
Ultramarine 108. Mark 33 in
blue.

15. Plate *d.* 20.3cm. Creamware.
Printed in blue, with slight enamelling
in orange. Bowpot pattern (1812-25).

SPODE

13. Barrel scent jar 35.5cm. *h.* Pearlware. Printed in
Ultramarine 108. Mark 33 in blue on base, and 132 on
perforated lid. *Courtesy Spode Museum.*

SPODE

SPODE

16. Comport on foot
29.3cm. *l.* Bone china.
Printed in Ultramarine
108. Mark in blue.

17. Plate *d.* 20.4cm. Pearlware. Printed in Ultramarine 108, enamelled in iron red with gilded tracing on the blue. Bowpot pattern with border sprays copied from the Chinese. Spode Pattern 2954.

18. Plate *d.* 22.9cm. Chinese porcelain. Painted in black and grey, with gilding on leaves and spearhead bead; the edge shows traces of gilding. *Courtesy Spode Museum.*

19. Plate *d.* 20.5cm. Stone china. Printed in blue, with gilding of pattern and brown edge. Marks in blue and in red. Bude pattern (1814-25).

20. Plate *d.* 22.4cm. Chinese porcelain, hand painted.

Grasshopper

This must have been a very popular pattern, while the border was used on many occasions with different centres. It has even been used with a Willow pattern centre. It is sometimes known as Grasshopper and Partridge (Fig. 21) and the Ch'ien Lung original can be dated about 1770 (Fig. 22).

21. Plate *d*. 24.2cm. Stone china, with mark in blue (*c*. 1812). Grasshopper pattern.

Stone·China

22. Plate *d*. 24.6cm. Chinese porcelain. Painted in blue. Ch'ien Lung (*c*. 1770).

23. Plate *d*. 24.9cm. Pearlware. Printed in Ultramarine 1 0 8. (1815-25). Lange Lijzen pattern.

SPODE

24. Plate *d*. 23.4cm. Chinese porcelain. Painted in Cyanine 1 0 5. Also has painted sprays on the back. K'ang Hsi or Ch'ien Lung.

Lange Lijzen

S.B. Williams credits the Dutch with giving the pattern (Fig. 23) this name which means 'slender damsel'. Some English people used to refer to the pattern as Long Eliza. The Chinese pattern dates from K'ang Hsi period, 1700-22, although the example illustrated (Fig. 24) may be from the Ch'ien Lung period. The leg bath illustrated (Fig. 25) is one of the most interesting examples of medical ceramics made on Spode's factory.

26. Plate *d.* 25.3 cm. Pearlware. Printed in blue. India pattern.

25. Leg bath 44.5 cm. Pearlware. *Courtesy Spode Museum.*

27. Plate *d.* 22.5 cm. Chinese porcelain. Painted in blue. K'ang Hsi period 1700-22.

India

Another Spode design (Fig. 26) reproducing K'ang Hsi porcelain (Figs. 27 and 28). Considerable quantities of India pattern must have been made as it is not rare and there are many engravings in the Spode copper plate store. It was introduced by Spode about 1815 with the earliest enamelled version having number 2489. Examples of India pattern are known with the printed inscription on the back which is referred to in Chapter 3.

Dragons No. 1

Introduced in about 1815 this is one of three Dragons patterns (Figs. 29 and 30), an enamelled version in green being recorded as Pattern 2414.

Dragons No. 2

The piece illustrated (Fig. 31) is very rare, but in the 1864 Print Record Book the number 2 is written beside it, though it is not known if the pattern was known then by the name Dragons No. 2. The design of the third Dragons pattern suggests that it was an outline print intended for an enamelled version.

Group

This has such an authentic Chinese appearance that it should be associated with the reproductions. Indeed Howard illustrates a Chinese porcelain lid with the arms of Johnstone with border decoration closely resembling Group pattern; this is in the style of the Ch'ien Lung period 1750-60. Whiter dates the introduction of the Spode pattern about 1809 when the first pattern number is 1437. Normally on pearlware (Figs. 32 and 33) it has also been made on stone china. (See Fence, and Peplow patterns.)

Chinese Flowers

Although rarely seen as a plain blue print, several examples are known (Fig. 34). The more usual versions are printed in a darker blue, enamelled and gilded. The earliest pattern number recorded is 2486, c. 1815. A Chinese porcelain example is in coral red (iron oxide) with gilding which the Dutch call 'milk and blood'. The flowers are chrysanthemum on the left and right with a Chinese variety of orchid, or a hemerocallis (day lily) in the middle.[51]

28. Reverse of plate in fig. 27.

29. Plate d. 23.3cm. Bone china.
Printed in Ultramarine 1 0 8. (c. 1815).
Dragons No. 1 pattern.   S P O D E

Spode

30. Stand for egg cups *d.* 18cm. Bone china. Printed in Ultramarine 1 0 8.

SPODE

31. Cup and saucer. Bone china. Printed in pale Ultramarine 1 0 8. Dragons No. 2 pattern.

Spode

32. Footed comport 30.3cm. *l.* Pearlware. Printed in Ultramarine 1 0 8. Group pattern.

33. Group pattern. *Courtesy Spode Museum.*

34. Covered muffin base *d.* 19.6cm. Pearlware. Outline
printed in blue. Chinese Flowers pattern (*c.* 1815).

SPODE

16 Spode patterns in the oriental style – non-landscape

This section includes those patterns for which an oriental original is not definitely identifiable. The patterns are Japan, Lily, Gloucester, Peplow, Lyre, Bamboo, Old Peacock, Spode's Phoenix, Ship and Star, 282 border, and Jar and Scroll. Two other patterns, for which no oriental original can be expected, are grouped here: Chinese Plants and Chinese of Rank.

Japan

A delicate pattern which S.B. Williams called Two Birds, but which in the 1864 print record book is named Japan. Jewitt lists New Japan, 1815, and Panel Japan, 1820. See figure 1.

4. Custard cup 7.6cm. *h.* Pearlware. Printed in Cyanine 105. Diagonal mark in blue, also a small ring turned in the base. Gloucester pattern. Attributed to Spode (*c.* 1800).

Lily

The earliest pattern to have its name, Lilley, recorded in the pattern book, written on a cup with a painted red bead at edge as pattern number 448, c. 1803 (Fig. 2). A cup in the Spode museum is with a Worcester saucer, but it seems likely that several items of teaware were made and not just the occasional replacement (Fig. 3).

Gloucester

There are several engravings in the Spode copper plate store that are very early in style, and the objects illustrated here also suggest that the pattern was produced in the last decade of the eighteenth century. An enamelled version with gilded sprays alternating with the printed ones is recorded as pattern number 1866, c. 1811. The name Gloucester was given to the pattern when it was reintroduced about 1929; this version includes a scroll bead around the centre which does not occur on the old pattern and, although the bead itself is Chinese in style, the addition is not authentic. The pattern is still in production at the Spode factory, and figures 4 to 6 show early nineteenth-century examples.

Peplow

Whiter illustrates an hexagonal shape plate in earthenware, while an oval dish in stone china is illustrated here (Fig. 7) which might be compared to Spode's Fence pattern.

There are several old engravings of the pattern (Fig. 8) and enamelled versions using the centre with different borders occur from pattern number 3060, c. 1819, onwards on bone china and earthenware. Two of these were among patterns exclusively sold by Harrods Ltd, London, up to 1939. The name dates from this century.

1. Dish 32.5cm. *l.* White earthenware. Printed in
Royal 1 1 0. Mark impressed. 1815-20. Japan pattern.
Courtesy Spode Museum.

2. Painted record in Spode's earliest pattern book.
Courtesy Spode Museum.

3. Cream jug. Old Oval shape, 12.9cm. *l.* Pearlware.
Printed in Cyanine 1 0 5. Unmarked. Lily pattern.
Attributed to Spode, *c.* 1800.

Bamboo

The pattern is recorded as an on-glaze red print with gilded leaves number 1185 and sometimes examples of this are found with the special mark of the three feathers, believed to have been used on services supplied to HRH the Prince of Wales, who in 1806 had appointed Josiah Spode II 'Potter and English Porcelain Manufacturer to His Royal Highness'. Blue printed versions, also with gilded leaves, are known on earthenware (Fig. 9). Howard illustrates a plate with Bamboos, chrysanthemums and rock of similar style with a crest on the rim of Ch'ien Lung period, about 1755.

Ship and Star

The ship border derives its name from pattern number 3067 which has a Chinese style centre showing a British East Indiaman ship sailing away; the frame is in the style of Meissen. The border was used in scores of different ways, but, when used with the Star centre[97] is so far known only in blue with gold, pattern number 3702 (Fig. 13).

282 Border

This basket and stand (Fig. 11) is the only example known to me with the border only and printed in blue. However there are several copper plates engraved for items of dinnerware and it is not possible to say if this was regarded as a pattern in its own right.

Jar and Scroll

Only one piece in this pattern, for which no factory name exists, is known (Fig. 12), but not only is it recorded as pattern number 3873, datable to about 1825, but there are several copper plates engraved for dinnerware items. It is a heavy outline pattern filled in with cobalt blue by painting. The three interlocking lozenge-shapes help in recognising the border design.

Lyre

Whiter supposed correctly that this pattern was produced as a plain print because examples of tea and coffee ware have been found (Figs. 13 and 14). The design is reminiscent of the style of Chinese blue and white Ming wares of the fifteenth

5. Coffee cup *d.* 6.7 cm. Pearlware. Printed in blue, with gilded edge. Handle is extruded, not moulded. Diagonal mark in blue. Attributed to Spode.

9. Plate *d.* 20.3 cm. Creamware. Printed in blue, with bamboo stems and leaves painted in pale orange. Bamboo pattern (1806)1810).

SPODE

SPODE

SPODE

6. Footed comport 30.2cm. *l.*
Pearlware. Printed in Cyanine
1 0 5. An early shape, called
Devonia (1805-10).

SPODES
NEW·STONE

7. Deep dish 37.0cm. *l.* Stone
china. Printed in Ultramarine
1 0 8. Centre of Peplow pattern,
bead of Flying Pennant and
border of Group pattern.

8. Print on paper 32.1cm. *l.*
Peplow pattern. Name of the
coppersmith J. Harlow, Stoke on
the reverse of the engraving.

10. Soup plate *d.* 23.9cm. Stone china. Printed in Royal 110, with gilded edge and tracing on pattern. Copeland and Garrett 1833-35. (Ship border and Star centre).

12. Square bowl *d.* 21.5cm. Stone china. Printed outline in Cyanine 105 and painted with washes of blue with gilded edge. Jar and Scroll pattern.

14. (*left*) **Coffee pot** 26.2cm. *h.* Pearlware. Printed in pale Cyanine 105 with edge and lining in 'old gold' enamel colour. Plain handle but leaf embossment on base of spout. No grid. Mark DD in blue. (Appears to be an accidental duplication of a printer's mark D).

15. (*above*) **Saucer** *d.* 13.4cm. Pearlware. Printed in bright Royal 110, with thick gilded edges. Circled cross marks printed in blue. Attributed to Spode (1800-1805) Old Peacock pattern.

16. Tea cup and saucer, saucer *d*. 13.8cm. Pearlware. Printed in Royal 110 with gilded edge and stroke on handle. Mark on cup in blue. Attributed to Spode (1800-1805). Lyre pattern.

11. Basket and stand, basket 5.6cm. *h*., stand 22.3cm. *l*. Bone china. Printed in Cyanine/Royal 105/110, with the border of pattern 282.

SPODE

century especially of the Ch'êng Hua period (1465-1487).[19]

Old Peacock

The pattern which bears this name in the Spode factory print record book of 1864 is not the same as that described by Williams and Whiter. Crosby Forbes,[51] founder-curator of the Museum of the American China Trade in Milton, Mass., suggests that the birds shown in Old Peacock pattern, illustrated here as in the print record book, would have been considered by the Chinese to be peacocks. In view of this, the name Old Peacock is here given to some recently found examples of the pattern (Fig. 15), which was probably produced about 1805 to 1810, at a time when the name SPODE was seldom applied to the ware but when the workman's mark was printed and no longer painted.

Spode's Phoenix

This is the pattern (Fig. 16) which Williams and Whiter called Old Peacock, but which is not named at all in the print record book. H.A. Crosby Forbes[51] considers that the birds in this pattern correspond to the Japanese convention for a phoenix. On this evidence, the name of the pattern should be changed to Spode's Phoenix. It is scarce and dates from 1815 to 1825. The design might be derived from a Japanese porcelain plate made at the Arita kilns for the Dutch East India Company 1658-83, and the birds might be ho-ho birds, or phoenixes. Crosby Forbes refers to C.S. Woodward (1974) *Oriental Ceramics at the Cape of Good Hope, 1652-1795,* Capetown and Rotterdam: A.A. Balkema, p.52, fig.83. He explains that while phoenixes have crested heads, generally cranes do not.

Chinese Plants

This pattern (Fig. 17) is included to show the change in fashion that occurred at the time when Copeland & Garrett took over the Spode business in 1833. This pattern, now called Aster which as a pink print and coloured underglaze is still produced by the Spode factory, dates to that time and represents a change of direction in representing oriental inspired design.

A Chinese of Rank

Felicity Mallet recognized[120] the source for this pattern as that entitled 'A Chinese of Rank' in the collection of aquatints in *A Picturesque Voyage to India by the way of China,* by Thomas and William Daniell, published in London in 1810. Since confirming the attribution by the presence of a copper plate (Fig. 18) and an egg stand marked SPODE (Fig. 19), several more engravings have been found, suggesting that a variety of objects were made (Fig. 20).

Borders of other patterns

Two of the best known blue-printed patterns of Spode are Blue Italian (Fig. 21) and Castle (Fig. 22). The inspiration for the border of Italian was undoubtedly a Chinese Imari design like that illustrated (Fig. 23), while it is probable that the border for Castle had a similar origin.

Other manufacturers' landscape patterns

Spode's designs were closest to the Chinese feeling because he was copying them with the purpose of providing matching pieces. His competitors when they were not doing the same thing, invented designs which should more correctly called chinoiserie patterns. A selection of these is illustrated here even though many of them are not yet attributed. (Figs. 24 to 39.)

17. Plate *d.* 25.9cm. White earthenware. Printed in pale Ultramarine 1 0 5. Chinese Plants pattern.

20. Saucer *d.* 13.9cm. Pearlware. Printed in Royal 1 1 0. Attributed to Spode (1800-1805).

19. Stand for egg cups *d.* 18.7cm. Pearlware. Printed in Ultramarine 1 0 8 (1805-10). Chinese of Rank pattern.

18. Print on paper from one of several engravings in the Spode Museum.

SPODE

SPODE

16. (*left*) **Plate** *d.* 25.0cm. Pearlware. Printed in Ultramarine 1 0 8. Spode's Phoenix pattern. (1820-1830).

23. Plate *d*. 23.2 cm. Chinese porcelain. Printed in red and other colours and gilded.

22. Plate *d*. 25.0 cm. Pearlware. Printed in Ultramarine 108. Spode's Castle (1820-25).

21. Plate *d*. 25.0 cm. Pearlware. Printed in Ultramarine 108. Blue Italian pattern (1820-30). SPODE

24. Items of teaware Saucer *d.* 12.9cm. Pearlware.
Printed in Ultramarine/Royal 1 0 8 / 1 1 0. Unmarked. Shown
with print on paper from a copper plate in the Spode collection.

25. Dish 48.0cm. *l.* Pearlware. Printed in
Cyanine 1 0 5. Mark 18 impressed.

26. Bowl *d.* 25.9cm. Pearlware.
Printed in Royal 1 1 0. Circled dot
mark.

27. Plate *d.* 24.5cm. Pearlware.
Printed in Cyanine 1 0 5. Unmarked.
Attributed to Davenport.

28. Plate *d.* 2.2cm. Pearlware.
Printed in blue. Unmarked.

29. Plate *d.* 24.9cm. Pearlware.
Printed in Cyaninc. Mark TURNER
impressed.

30. Saucer *d.* 13.4cm. Porcelain.
Printed in Cyanine 1 0 5. Unmarked.

31. Jug 12.9cm. *h.* Pearlware.

33. Cup and saucer saucer *d.* 13.2cm. Pearlware. Printed in dark blue. Unmarked.

32. Cup and saucer, saucer *d.* 14.0cm. Porcelain. Printed in Cyanine 1 0 5, with painted shading and broad gilded edge. Unmarked. Attributed to New Hall.

34. Plate *d.* 23.0cm. Pearlware. Printed in blue. Unmarked.

35. Plate *d.* 23.8cm. Pearlware. Printed in blue. Mark impressed.

36. Plate *d.* 19.0cm. Porcelain. Printed in dark blue with gilded edge and line below border. Unmarked. Probably Caughley.

37. Sauce tureen stand 19.6cm. *l.* Pearlware. Printed in Royal 1 1 0. X mark.

41. Jug 19.3cm. *h.* Pearlware. Printed in dark blue. Unmarked.

39. Vase 19.3cm. *h.* Pearlware. Printed in blue. Unmarked. Possibly Leeds.

Comparative names of Spode patterns

	WHITER	COYSH I 1970 COYSH II 1972	DES FONTAINES[48]	OTHERS
WILLOW I	Willow, 'First'			Willow (S B Williams)
WILLOW II	Willow, 'Second'			True Willow (Godden)
WILLOW III	Willow, 'Third'	Standard Willow (I)	Standard Willow	Willow (Little) British-Nankin, Coalport (Godden)
MANDARIN I pearlware	–			Willow-Nankin, Caughley porcelain (Godden)
MANDARIN II bone china	Dagger-Landscape, Third			Willow-type (S B Williams) Two birds in flight, pavilion,
MANDARIN III stone china	–			and Willow (Crosby-Forbes)
ROCK I pearlware	Rock			Rock, moored vessel and
ROCK II bone china	–			Willow (Crosby-Forbes)
TWO FIGURES I	–			
TWO FIGURES II	Two Figures	Caughley Willow	Willow-type	
PEARL RIVER HOUSE	–			Malayan Village (Copeland ECC) Trench Mortar (Watney)
TWO TEMPLES I, var Temple	Temple			Two Temples (Williams-Wood) Willow or Temple (S B Williams)
TWO TEMPLES II, var Broseley	Broseley	Broseley (II) Two man/insect (I)		Pagoda (Godden) Willow (Little)
BRIDGE I pearlware	–	Queen Charlotte (II) One man chinoiserie (I)		
BRIDGE II bone china	Queen Charlotte			
NEW BRIDGE stone china	–			
LAKE	Dagger-Landscape Second			
TEMPLE-LANDSCAPE I	–			Inclined pines and Banana
TEMPLE-LANDSCAPE II	Temple-Landscape, Second			palm (Crosby-Forbes)
TEMPLE-LANDSCAPE var. Parasol	Parasol Figure			Willow with one man on bridge & covered boat (S B Williams)
BUDDLEIA	Temple-Landscape, First.			Early Willow (Little)
BUNGALOW				
FOREST LANDSCAPE I	Forest-Landscape, First.	Chinoiserie (I)		Willow-type (S B Williams)
FOREST LANDSCAPE II	Forest-Landscape, Second		Willow-type	
TEMPLE WITH PANEL	Dagger-Landscape, First			
FLYING PENNANT	Flying Pennant	Two man/two arch (I)	Willow-type	Flying streamer (S B Williams)
TALL DOOR	Tall Door			
UNKNOWN UCL I	–			
UNKNOWN UCL II				
UNKNOWN UCL III		Two man/insect (I)	Willow type	Willow-type (Godden)
LONG BRIDGE		Two man/scroll (I)		Swansea Willow (M Nance)
TROPHIES-NANKIN	Trophies-Nankin	Hundred Antiques (I)		
TROPHIES-ETRUSCAN	Trophies-Etruscan		Hundred Antiques	Hundred Antiques (S B Williams)
TROPHIES-DAGGER	–			
TROPHIES MARBLE	–		Hundred Antiques/ Cracked Ice	
FITZHUGH	Trophies Dagger		Fitzhugh	
BUFFALO	Buffalo	Buffalo (I)	Water Buffalo	

	WHITER	WILLIAMS	DES FONTAINES	
GRASSHOPPER	Grasshopper	Bird and Grasshopper	Grasshopper	Bird and Grasshopper (Coysh)
LANGE LIJZEN	Lanje Lijzen	Lange Lijsen	Jumping Boy	
SPODE'S PHOENIX	Old Peacock	Old Peacock		
JAPAN	Japan	Two Birds		
DRAGONS I	Dragons	Chinese Dragon		

APPENDIX I : TEA CONSUMPTION AND TAXATION

Some idea of the huge quantities of Chinese blue and white porcelain shipped to England in the eighteenth century may be obtained from studying a contract which was made with Sinqua, the Chinese Hong merchant, on 19 August 1772 for chinaware 'to be delivered early for the Ships of next Season' in the quantities as follows:

		Pattern		Ta^e	mcc	£	s	d
350	Table Services, long dishes, blue & white (ea. 18 dishes 8 to 18in, 60 plates, 20 soup plates, 1 tureen to 2 sets).	7	set	12	600	4	4	0
100	Table Services, round dishes, blue & white 80 plates, 1 tureen to 4 sets.	2	set	10		3	6	8
300	Sets of Salad dishes, 4 of sizes 9 to 11ins.	3	set		600		4	0
45	Bowls, size 2 gallons	2	Each	1			6	8
45	Bowls, size 1½ gallons	2			800		5	4
105	Bowls, size 4 quarts	2			300		2	0
300	Bowls, size 3 quarts	3			250		1	8
900	Bowls, size 2 quarts	3			150		1	0
1650	Bowls, size 3 pints	3			120			9½
2550	Bowls, size 1 quart	3			090			7
3150	Bowls, size 1½ pints	3			070			6
16000	Basons, size 1 pint	6			048			4
20000	Basons, size ½ pint	6			034			3
5000	Breakfast cups & saucers	3	pair		075			6
80000	Single plates blue & white	6	Each		033			3
2000	Soup plates	2			043			4
5000	Flat water plates	3			024			2
8100	Deep water saucers	3			026			2
1800	Sugar dishes and tops	3			070			6
7500	Coffee cans	3			014			1
1050	Tea pots	3			100			8
750	Milk ewers	3			100			8
750	Sets of 3 Patty pans	3	Set		150		1	0
360	Tea Services, 43 pieces each	4	Set	1			6	8
39000	Large tea cups and saucers	7	Each		042			4
87000	Small tea cups and saucers	7			026			2
2400	Sets of long dishes, 10, 11 and 12ins.	4	Set		550		3	8
600	Sets of round dishes	2	Set		450		3	0

Source: India Office Records R/10/9 Page 41. China Factory Records. Consultations 1771-72.[119] Also referred to by Morse.[130]

Note: The £ s d values are not on the original document

The figures were not totalled and there is no obvious reference to a total, although one may have been mentioned later when payment was made. A recent check gives a total of Taels 17806, or £5,935.6.8d. Morse's total of Taels 17780 would be valued at £5,926.13.4d. The quantity of ware was about 485,000 separate pieces. Morse states that in 1775 five ships visited Canton and nine ships in 1777, each ship taking 1200-1800 Taels of chinaware.[126] Comparing these details with the sale proceeds of chinaware in London, in 1773 (Company sales £36,079, Private £19,332) and in 1774 (Company sales £24,083, Private £14225) suggests that the sale price in London was about four times cost price in Canton.

The East India Company were not buying chinaware primarily for resale but as floorings for tea, and the trade was conducted without figuring the loss. The private trade was much on the ordinary lines. The following examples were quoted by Morse:

Fox Captain: Hyson tea, 100 chests; Chinaware, 95 half chests, boxes and rolls; Lacquered ware, 4 boxes. *Officers:* Hyson, 44 chests; Chinaware, 53 boxes.

London Captain: Hyson, 90 chests; Chinaware, l6 boxes and tubs; Lacquered ware, 6 cases; Paper prints, painted glass, images, 8 cases; Soy, 1 cask; sweetmeats, 3 boxes; Madeira, 2 pipes, 1 chest. *Officers:* Hyson, 30 chests; Chinaware, 30 boxes and tubs; Lacquered ware, prints and sundries, 25 chests.

Bohea tea was packed in chests lined with lead, or spelter (zinc), which were soldered at the joints to render the inside water and air tight. The largest chest weighed 350-360 pounds and the smallest 60-70 pounds. By 1825 the various weights were 185, 108½ and 62 pounds respectively. Other teas were packed in smaller chests ranging from 93 to 67 pounds, but chests of 60 pounds were permitted. Morse states that in 1797 the Company's agent in Cape Town asked that one half of the tea consigned to him should be sent in 10 catty boxes. A catty was 1⅓ pounds weight. In 1825 the Americans, in filling indents for Quebec and Halifax, asked that certain quantities of Hyson and young Hyson tea be sent in smaller packages – 3,000 boxes of 10 catties and 2,380 boxes of 25 catties – partly to satisfy the demands of the market but chiefly as being more convenient for loading ships and boats of small size.[119] (See fig. 2 of Chapter 1)

Average figures for the basic cost of tea per pound, and the rates of tax thereon, in various years, obscure several factors. For example, there were considerable differences of price between the highest and lowest grades of tea: the higher grades paid an additional tax. But taking this into account, the relationship between the price and tax in certain representative years may be tabled.

	Average price paid without Tax		Tax paid		Total price	
	s	d	s	d	s	d
1772	3	6¼	4	6	8	0¼
1782	3	5½	2	2½	5	7½
1783	3	9	2	4	6	1
1786	3	3		5	3	8
1790	3	1½		5	3	6½
1796	2	8		8¼	3	4¼
1800	3	1¼	1	3	4	4¼
1809	3	5	2	9½	6	2½

This table shows that the Commutation Act had a marked and beneficial effect on the price of tea for about ten years[143] before the financial necessities imposed by the Napoleonic Wars caused taxation to be increased once more.[119]

TABLE I

SALES OF TEA COMPARED TO TOTAL IMPORTS

	HEIC SALES		*Proceeds*	*Duty Paid*	*TOTAL IMPORTS*
	including re-exports	*less re-exports*	*HEIC & Private*		*retained for Home*
	lbs. wt.	*lbs.*	*£*	*£*	*Consumption. lbs. wt.*
1771	6,814,661	5,566,793	1,313,705	317,635	
1779	6,660,704		1,211,547	702,307	
1780	7,577,879		1,312,397	731,035	
1781	5,031,649	4,915,472	1,008,671	705,535	12,000,000 (estimate)
1782	6,495,518		1,289,896	719,801	
1783	5,877,340		1,113,375	682,965	
1784	9,937,248		2,505,368	380,761	
1785	14,921,893		2,195,696	298,194	
1786	15,943,682		2,585,803	314,946	
1787	16,222,923		2,401,295	316,646	
1791	17,268,317	15,096,840	2,403,338	344,293	
1801	24,531,514		3,570,149	1,554,152	23,730,000
1811	23,040,990			3,189,225	22,455,000
1821					26,755,000
1831				* Excise duty was paid	29,997,000
1841				in addition to Customs	36,676,000
1841				so more than doubling	36,676,000
				the tax.	

Source, HEIC Records
L/AG/10/2 & 18/2
and Wissett.
S J McNally.

Source, H.M. Customs
& Excise cited by
Forrest. pp. 284 & 285.

Note 1. Disparity between the figures is due to the HEIC records including re exports, while HM Customs & Excise statistics exclude them.

Note 2. Imports of tea remained steady from 1801-1831, despite the re-imposition of heavy duties which reverted to as much as 90% in 1806.

TABLE II

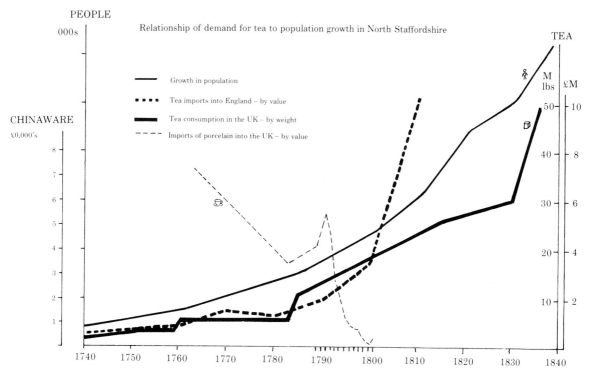

PEOPLE
000s

Relationship of demand for tea to population growth in North Staffordshire

TEA

——— Growth in population

■ ■ ■ ■ Tea imports into England – by value

▬▬▬ Tea consumption in the UK – by weight

– – – Imports of porcelain into the UK – by value

CHINAWARE
£0,000's

M lbs   £M

APPENDIX II : THE PRODUCTION OF COBALT

In view of the importance for ceramic history of Schindler's description of the production and use of cobalt, his text is given almost in full[4]:

Two miles below Kamsar some thin lodes of copper ore crop out in shales which dip 80° west, and strike north 22°west to south 22° east. One mile or less north of the copper lodes are the celebrated cobalt mines which have been worked in ancient times, and belong to some sayyids of Kamsar and Kashan. The rocks there are dolomites broken through by serpentines with an immense lode of iron ore, copper pyrites, sulphuret of nickel, cobalt bloom, and earthy cobalt (peroxide). The lode strikes north 7° west to south 7° east, and dips 80° west. Only the earthy cobalt is at present of any practical value; it contains about five per cent of metal. It is collected by the proprietors and washed with water, and the heavy sediment is made into cakes. The washing process is called *saravabuna* i.e. sar i ab va bun i ab (top water and bottom water). The cakes, under the name of lajverd i Kashi, are exported, principally to Kashan, Qum, and Isfahan, where they are sold at the rate of about one shilling and sixpence per pound. All the proprietors receive equal shares of the proceeds, and they have an agent (bonek-dar) who looks after the sale and keeps account for them for a commission. In order not to lower the price only a certain quantity, sufficient for the actual demand, about 1300lbs per annum, is put on the market, and should there not be a demand for this quantity, the mine is closed and carefully guarded.

The ore is reduced in the following way: ten parts by weight of the earth or ore (in cakes), five of potash (keliab), five of borax (burch), are pounded together to a fine powder, and then made into a paste with grape treacle (shirch), and formed into small balls or cakes. The balls are then put with pounded quartz into a *sufar* (earthen pot with wide opening) and exposed to heat in a furnace for sixteen hours. The metal gained in this way amounts to about one twentieth of the weight of the cobalt cakes employed.

To use the cobalt for colouring pottery it is ground into fine powder with an equal quantity of quartz. This powder is applied to gum *under the glaze* and is therefore called *zir rang* i.e. 'under-colour'. For painting over the glaze the metal is ground together with forty times its weight of rock crystal or old glass (that containing manganese is best) and twice its weight of borax, and the mixture, in an earthen pot, is exposed to heat in a furnace until the whole of it is deposited on the inside of the pot as a crust of blue glaze like glass. The blue crust is then separated from the pot, and is applied, ground into powder, to pottery with gum. Both these processes are very costly, and, calculating the cost of the cobalt cakes, of the borax, potash, quartz, fuel, furnace etc., the cost of the powder, ready for being used as colouring matter, amounts to 28 shillings per pound, by the first process, and to 38 shillings per pound by the second process. A cheaper way of preparing a blue colour is to pound one part of cobalt (metallic), with four parts of the cobalt cakes, into a fine powder, and applying powder *under the glaze*, but the colour obtained in this way is not good, and is employed only for very cheap pottery.

Ladame found the same cobalt compounds present in Qamsar. One must therefore assume that Abul-Qasim's 'white silver shining in a sheath of hard black stone' was asbolane, though such a description fits the sulpharsenide of cobalt, rather better. On the other hand, the ash-coloured and soft type from Farangistan (roughly Europe) sounds more like asbolane, which is essentially wad, consisting of up to 40% cobalt oxide. The red kind is clearly erythrite, which has a pinkish-violet colour, and being an arsenic compound (hydrated cobalt arsenate) is indeed a deadly poison.

Another important document concerns the development of smalts of cobalt. Christian Schurmer of Neudeck, Bohemia, in 1540 produced the double silicate of cobalt and potassium which resulted in *Smalts*. According to Bruchmueller the process was as follows:

This blue colour was made by taking the cobalt ore, in this case, Smaltite, ($CoAS_2$), which contained some bismuth, and melting the bismuth out by gentle heating; then it was stamped and roasted in reverberatory furnaces.[20] It was important that the roasting or oxidation should be as complete as possible. The result of this process was the cobalt oxide, known in the trade as safflor, a greyish brown powder. In order to make cobalt blue out of the oxide it is mixed with potassium carbonate (pearl ash) and white quartz and fused, then dipped out with iron spoons into a large vat, in which cold water runs continuously. By this means the blue coloured glass attained its deep blue tint and became so brittle that it could be crushed and ground (the blue colour or *smalt* usually contained about 6% cobalt. This crushed and ground material is then sifted, washed and finally graded through very fine sieves. By means of the washing the soluble constituents are removed and the different colours known to the trade are produced, according to the fineness of the material.

The importance of Scandanavian imports is shown by the fact that in 1799 John Leslie wrote to Josiah Wedgwood II with samples of Swedish cobalt:

'Inclosed are specimens of Crystalized Cobalt which were given me by a gentleman in Stockholm, intimately connected with the mines. At my request he marked the prices at which it could be supplied all charges included. If it should answer your purpose he will engage to furnish it in considerable quantities. The price appears to be more moderate than what I have heard before and I hope to render a service to the manufactory of Etruria in promoting the contract. I spent a day with the gentleman and from what I could perceive and learn he is a person of worth. The Swedish paper dollar is about three shillings in value and the pound weight is nearly the same as the English. He thinks that it would be perhaps preferable to send the pure oxyd of cobalt (of a rose colour) prepared by solution and precipitation and which would be liable to less uncertainty. This he could afford at 9 dollars per lb. I shall send it with other specimens to Mr Byerley.[110]

Preparation of Blues

All the best blues are made with the crystallized cobalt of Sweden. Take it as it comes from the mines, pulverize it and dissolve it by Aqua Fortis in a captula on a sand bath; the solution is then of a wine colour decanted off from the sediment that cannot be dissolved, but in what you have decanted, the double quantity of its weight of river water then filter it through a gray paper, drop into it a liacuratum of very pure and filtered potash; then makes a yellowish white precipitate. It is necessary at first to put a small quantity of potash to cause the first precipitate, when it is well deposited the supernatant liquor has a reddish lilac colour, decant it and filter it, after which add to it some more potash till it ceases to form a fresh precipitate which is purple or rose colour, it is this second precipitate that contains the fine blue. The first holds nothing but iron and nickle etc (*sic*) and of course is good for nothing. Wash well with warm water the precipitate which contains the blue (the second) then filter it and dry it betwixt biscuit plates and keep it for use. This is called nitrate of cobalt.

Dry Way of Preparing Blue

Wash the cobalt and calcine it in the open air to take out the arsenic, mix the oxide with three times its weight of black flux and calcine it in a crucible (the black flux is the result of the combustion of two parts of tartar and one part nitre, as there is no equal part of substances the quantity of nitre which is in the flux not being sufficient to consume all the carbonic matter of the tartar the mass resulting from that combustion is loaded with much of that carbonic matter quite black which gives it the name of Black Flux). Warm slightly in a crucible the mineral cobalt and when you see it has ceased burning increase your fire till the matter is fluxed, let the crucible go cold and break it; you will then divide the cobalt that you will find in a mass from the Scoria that are always blue, the cobalt thus reduced contains always a small quantity of iron unless the mineral is of a superfine quality, then the metal obtained has the colour of iron, is brittle and heavy and will resemble collected needles in its fracture. N.B. The Blue Makers generally mix Zaffre with two or three times its weight of sand to make it go further (for Painting Blues ought to be made by the humid or wet way.)

Various Recipes for the Making of Blue

Process 59
To make a Blue printed Flux
Take 2 parts of flint
1 of process 32 and ½ part flint glass.

Process 60
To Make a Blue printed Flux
Take 5 parts of flint
1½ of Borax   ½ of Nitre

Process 61
To make a painting and Edging Blue
Take 2 of blue calx   3 of frit Process 32
1½ of flint glass   1 of flint
½ of white lead

Process 62
For a Strong Blue
2 of blue calx   3 of Printing Flux 58 or 59 Processes

Process 63
To make a printing Broseley Blue
Take 1 of blue calx, 4 of printing flux 60

These several processes are essentially connected with each other and have the attainment of one of the same object or purpose in view, therefore classed in regular succession. The Frit No. 32 should be prepared without the oxide of tin when mixed with the blue calx for that metal and arsenic are both prejudicial to its colour; plaster and flint may be substituted for the preparation of printing blue, but when ground and dried it immediately assumes a stone-like hardness very light in its specific gravity and imbibes an excess of oil before it is in a proper state for use on trial or by experiment. The colour will be perceptibly weaker or lighter than blue calx when mixed with a calcined high vitreous flux in the same ratio the density and compactness of the latter causes it more easily to enter the engraved parts of the copper plate so that a great body of blue is of course transferable and readily contained on the biscuit pieces of ware, consequently the colour, when glazed and fired, will appear stronger. The two following mixtures are receipts for printers oil with proper directions for preparing the same, for some oils which are made use of prove injurious to the tint of the Blues. Zaffre blue may be mixed in equal parts with cobalt blue and the colour will nevertheless be good blue for the coarser sort of Earthenware. Zaffre blue is generally used above.

Process 64
To make a Printers Oil
Take 1 quart of Linseed Oil
1 pint of rape oil
2oz of Balsam capivi
1oz of pitch
½oz Amber oil
½oz of White lead

Process 65
To make Printers Oil
1 Quart of Linseed Oil
¼pt of rape oil   ¼pt Common Tar
1oz of Balsam of Sulphur
1oz of Balsam of Capivi

Method

The principal object in preparing these oils is the care required in adding the different ingredients at the proper times. First the linseed oil should be boiled for sometime alone then may be added the rape oil and the balsam of capivi, after which allow the boiling to be continued until it begins to approach the proper consistency, which is known by taking out at intervals a small quantity. Then may be added the remaining ingredients but the mixture should be allowed to cool a short time after which the whole mass may be boiled slowly until it has assumed the proper thickness. Let it be observed that the vessel must be generally covered during the process and the sulphur previously to be mixed with the oil should be pulverized as by that means it is less liable to make the oil curdle or coagulate.

Process 66
To make a Blue stain
Take 5 parts of Blue calx.   2 of Frit Process 32
1 of flint glass   1 of Enamel blue

In the foregoing enamel fluxes the materials are to be made very fine particularly the flint, and mixed well together so that the particles may more easily concrete when in a state of fusion. The calcine in an air furnace or an earthenware glazing oven when the whole mass by means of the proper temperature of fire will be changed into a brittle resplendent and transparent glass.

Process 74
To make smalts blue
Take 32 sand, 32 of potash
10 of Borax and one of Blue calx.
These smalts, materials of which are calcined in the usual manner when finally pulverized will produce fine rich looking blue powder.

Process 108
To Procure the Regulus of Zaffre
(Regulus is a mass of partly purified ore, or the product of smelting ore). Take 112 parts of Zaffre, 57 parts of Potash, 18½ parts of charcoal. This is the first process towards making blue calx and is called 'running down', but more properly smelting. The charcoal being pulverized and all the materials mixed up together and afterwards put into large crucibles capable of holding from three to four quarts and filled quite full, then placed in a strong brick built reverberatory furnace commencing with a slow fire and continuing for sometime but as soon as it is heated to a red heat it will require a considerably stronger fire before the cohesion between the different articles is sufficiently destroyed. This operation will be complete in about 10 hours the weight of the regulus being from 31-33lbs: on examining the scoria, if there remain mixed with it small pieces of metal not much unlike small shot and when pounded, if the scoria has a bluish cast it is an ocular demonstration that the fire has not been strong enough; there is little danger to be apprehended from the most intense heat provided the particles in fusion do not perforate the crucibles which are made of a mixture of marls with a little sand; at the bottom of each cake of regulus there will be bismuth slightly adhering which is easily separated without any degree of heat by placing the cakes upon an Iron Plate or pane which will soon bring the bismuth into a liquid state and separate from the regulus.

Process 109
To refine the regulus of Zaffres
Take 50 parts of regulus, 6 parts of potash, 3 parts of sand. When the regulus is deprived of its bismuth and pulverized it is to be well mixed with a quantity of potash and sand as before mentioned, then put into smaller crucibles holding about 1½lbs each, fired in a reverberatory furnace commencing with a slow fire and gradually increasing for about the space of 8 hours. By that time the regulus will have fallen to the bottom of the crucible and the scoria found at the top will be of a blackish green, therefore it will be indispensably necessary that another course of refining should take place in order that the regulus may be obtained in a more perfect state of purity.

Process 110
To refine the regulus of Zaffre a second time
Take 50 parts of refined regulus, 6 parts of potash, 3 parts of sand. These materials to be mixed fired and treated in every respect the same as in the former process of refining but a further fusion is required in order to purge the sulphurous parts which adhere to the metal and which in consequence of the fluxes attracting and absorbing it if frequently found mixed with the scoria, the regulus will then be sufficiently purified for the next operation.

Process 111
To procure pure calx from refined regulus of Zaffre
To 30 parts of refined regulus of Zaffre, 1 part of plaster, ½ part Borax, these materials made very fine and exceedingly well mixed up together, after which put the mixture into Earthenware biscuit cups made 1½ inches high, 3 inches diameter and half an inch thick, filled nearly to the top. Set them in a reverberatory furnace, the fire to be increased until the mixture is perceived to be in a state of fusion; the same degree of heat must be continued for about 6 hours afterwards and then the fire hastily slackened. This operation of calcining will occupy from 12-13 hours; at the top of the cups will be found a blue calx separated from the nickel but as a large portion of blue will still remain in the nickel when sunk to the bottom of the cups it will be necessary in order to procure the whole of the blue contained to pursue precisely the same method over again, namely the metal mixed up with the plaster and borax and calcined in the same manner as described before, and then without doubt it will yield all the remainder of the blue, which will be found as before at the top of the cups and the nickle (*sic*) sunk to the bottom, the blue calx obtained by the first process is the best and purest, however, the first and second as they are called are mixed together and sold under the appellation of Zaffre Blue.

Process 112
To make Cobalt Blue
Take 60 parts of cobalt ore, 50 parts of potash, 25 parts of sand, 10 parts of charcoal. Let these materials be well mixed together and put in crucibles considerably smaller than those adopted for the smelting of Zaffres. About 1½lbs of this mixture will be sufficient in each crucible and the remaining part of the processes are the same in every respect and to be attended to in the same way as described in the process for smelting Zaffres when regulus of cobalt will be obtained.

Process 113
To refine regulus of cobalt
Take 50 parts of regulus, 6 parts of potash, the regulus must be pulverized and mixed up with the other materials. Instead of using crucibles as in refining the regulus of Zaffres they should be earthenware cupels in the shape of the old pickle jars or bottles with flange tops, they contain one lb of the mixture. Cobalt ores vary very much in the quantity and quality of blue they contain whether the ore be poor or rich the same process is to be adopted. The operation of refining must be as often repeated as is necessary, that is, until the scoria is of a bright colour and of a slight bluish hue which requires in general about 3 times and in some instances 5 times refining before the regulus is sufficiently purged and purified for the next operation.

Process 114
To roast refined regulus of cobalt
This process is performed by spreading the purified metal finely pulverized half an inch thick on flat pieces of earthenware covered with flint and placed in a reverberatory furnace, and a moderate degree of heat applied for a few hours. Care and observation will be particularly required that the metal by an excess of heat does not get into a state of liquifaction; if so, the object will be defeated, by expelling the arsenic which it contains. The metals from which the cobalt is with the greatest difficulty disengaged are arsenic and nickel; the former is effected by being exposed to a gentle heat which is called 'roasting', the latter by repeated fusion and calcining or calking.

Process 115
To procure pure calx from the refined regulus of cobalt.
Take 30 of refined regulus of cobalt, 1 of plaster, ½ of borax. The regulus, after being calcined which is also called 'roasting' is to be pulverized quite fine and completely mixed with the plaster and borax, and the same method strictly adopted and observed as that pursued in calking the refined regulus of Zaffres, and as both preparations are in reality perfectly alike consequently the operator cannot do better than refer to that process.

Summing up

Having thoroughly described the method of manufacturing cobalt and Zaffre blue through various and intricate processes, together with the mode of operation, it would be impossible to state the exact quantities of fire required in each operation for the effect of heat bears an exact proportion to the mass of the body, the size of the furnace and the strength of the fire employed. Zaffres are of a dark grey colour about the fineness of sand, and cobalt ores are of a grey colour shining hard and ponderous. Certain arsenical ores which are similar in appearance have frequently obtained the name of cobalt, but falsely; calx of cobalt and Zaffres dissolve in Marine acid in great abundance if the solution be green it is owing to the calx containing nickel, if it be pure the solution yields crystals of a fine red colour inclining to be blue.

The blue colours are supplied by the oxide of cobalt whose tendency to Alumine renders them the most rich, fine, solid and fixed whatever heat may be applied of all colours on porcelain or flint ware. The pure oxide is used for the very rich and beautiful tints; and for the other various combinations of the oxides of cobalt, tin and zinc. But much of the brilliance is dependent on the components of the body or the glaze as well as the variety of shades. The alkalies give a deep blue precipitate; fusion with an antimony and litharge forming a green, and fusion with iron and manganese a black. The alkaline earths, barytes, lime and magnesia effect the cobalt when sulphuric acid is present and injure or destroy the printed patterns. The oxide of cobalt should be completely freed from arsenic to prevent the radiation of the metal by its combination with the alumine of the body, resembling smeared wiring and injuring the lines which should be clear and distinct; or giving a bluish tint to the white glazed ware baked at the same time in the same saggar with blue painted or printed. Broignart first announced this remarkable effect and also, but without giving the process, that from pure chromate of lead he had obtained a fixed deep blue for porcelain, yet he has blamed his predecessors for the very same conduct.

Blue. Pulverize cobalt ore and mix well; Ore 40 carbonate of potass, 40, Lynn Sand 14, Charcoal 6. Alternatively Cobalt Ore 25 Zaffre 25, Potass 35, Sand 10, Charcoal 5. In crucibles that contain about 3 pints put 1½lbs of mixed material; place these in a muffle connected with a reverberatory furnace; gradually raise the heat for 7 hours, then regularly diminish for 9 hours longer. When cool the upper substance will be cobalt and a silicate of potass; and below will be nickel and bismuth.

Then pulverize the silicate and the powder put in small pint flanged biscuit jars; calx 90, potass 10; about 1lb in each crucible, raise the heat 6 hours and diminish 7. Repeat this till the silicate be a very pale colour, pulverize this calx also.

Next on biscuit dishes strew ground flint one quarter of an inch thick in which spread the last calx and carefully calcine well 6 hours to dissipate the arsenic (which will remain if the calx be fused) and separate the nickel. Pulverize the blue calx and mix well. Calx 90 best flint 6. borax 4: 85 calx. 9 flint. 6 potass.

In similar way mix like quantities of Zaffre and the alkalies to form a coarse blue. In earthen cups half an inch thick, 3 inches diameter and 1½ inch high put of the powder and place in a muffle. Raise the heat 6 hours and diminish 7 hours. The top will be blue calx, the bottom nickel and other metallic scoria. When a quantity of nickel is accumulated, pulverize and mix metal 80 plaster, 12 borax 8; put in cups and fuse 16 hours. The best blue thus obtained is usually mixed with the Zaffre blue.

Strong Blue (for printing)
Blue calx 40, flux 60. (Petuntze 80 potass 20) (or red lead 18 flint 36 glass 28 nitre 9 borax 9)
or calx 35 or 30 and flux 65 or 70.
or calx 20 flux 40 and white lead 40.
or calx 25 flint or barytes 35.
Weak brosley, blue calx 20, flux 80 (flint 70 nitre 9 borax 21).
or calx 15 petuntze 85.

Cobalt ores are found in several places in England, yet although there is so great a demand for the calx weekly they are not collected. A few years ago a Company for that purpose was formed and their produce sold at the average price of 47/6 per lb; but the prejudices of the potters and the want of chemical knowledge, neglect on how to procure pure calx from the refuse scoria rendered the concern unprofitable and Zaffres continue in demand for the preparation of the colour.

APPENDIX IV : MARKS

Few examples of early blue printed wares carry manufacturers' marks. This applies as much to Spode's production as to those of other manufacturers. It is possible that marks only began to be used as trade expanded and manufacturers needed to make their own product more prominent.

There are a number of alternative means available for attributing an unmarked piece. The factory may have records of printed patterns or engravings: the design of the pattern can be compared with that on a marked piece: other indications are the shape and finish of the piece, the quality of the workmanship, the standard of the colour printing and the tone and grade of blue.

No book can explain satisfactorily the feeling of a glaze, which distinguishes the wares of one factory from those of another. Neither is it easy to describe the differences in quality of workmanship; such knowledge is acquired mainly through the experience of handling objects. But what a book can do is to record what is known about those distinguishing features which are more visual than sensuous.

SHAPES. Because so little early domestic pottery survives, it is seldom possible to compare the shape of an article with an exactly similar one in the same pattern, but sometimes it may be done with one in a different pattern. It is often in small details, such as the shape of a handle or a knob that a distinguishing feature may be found. In teapots of similar appearance it may be a distinction of line of the body or the number of facets on a spout which is all-important.

Another form of mark that can help identification is the workman's mark. Sometimes these occur on early Spode wares. In 1975 Paul Holdway realised the significance of this type of mark which has been known for years but not appreciated until then; he recovered from a minor excavation on the Spode factory two pieces of a pattern with which he was unfamiliar. They proved to be of a pattern not previously realised as having been made by Spode but of which a photograph of a marked Spode dish had been sent to the author. Later, he bought six tea saucers whose pattern corresponded to that in the photograph, and which were marked with hand painted blue strokes. By examining other pieces of marked Spode pieces he found several with similar workmen's marks, and it is possible now to illustrate a wide range of such marks which occur on Spode pieces.

But workmen did not apply marks for the benefit of collectors! Workmen were paid on a piecework basis and, until 1872, on the work being satisfactory after it had been fired: 'good from oven' as it was called. It was essential, therefore, that the wares of a particular craftsman, or team in the case of transfer printing, could be identified after firing: the mark had to be indelible. Josiah Spode I was believed to 'have introduced blue printing into Stoke in 1784' so it is likely that his workmen were among the first to adopt simple marks, especially as his trade may have expanded faster than that of his local competitors. So far about thirty marks are known, suggesting that about this number of transfer printing teams may have been employed on the Spode factory.

These marks were applied by hand with a brush by the transferrer. Any printing team or craftsman on any factory could have used similar marks, so the presence on an object of a mark comparable to a Spode workman's mark can not be regarded as irrefutable evidence that the object was made on the Spode factory. The Spode workman might have moved, taking his mark with him, or another workman on another factory could have adopted the same or a closely similar mark. Later marks were printed on the ware from engraved copper plates, one for each printing team, of which twenty-four have been recorded to date.

Craftsmen in the clay making departments seem not to have marked their wares in the early days, judging from the absence of marks impressed in the clay. When the volume of production increased however, each maker would have needed to identify his work, and the numbers which occur below the later, and larger, capital letter mark of SPODE could well be clay makers' marks. Few patterns included in this book, however, come within the period of these particular later printed and impressed marks.

As to the availability of factory records, Spode did not record on paper patterns which were plain prints to which no painted or gilded adornment was added: only if a coloured edge, gold tracing, or other ornamentation which required a decorating kiln fire was added would a record of the pattern be made. None of the Chinese landscape patterns occur in the pattern books: this is doubly unfortunate in that patterns were entered in chronological order, and entries would have provided a guide to dating.

Impressed Marks

1a	SPODE	**c1785-90** An early mark which has been seen on a dish of Two Figures pattern (Whiter Plate 3).
1d	SPODE	**c1785-90** Mark 1d occurs on a blue painted drainer, items of a dessert set and on very early versions of Two Figures pattern.
2a	SPODE	**c1790-1802** Always neat and varying in size from 8–10mm. Found usually on early printed wares but also on very early bone china and dry bodies.
2b	SPODE	Somewhat larger than Mark 2a, 11–44mm, and occasionally found with a slight curve. Usually appears on dry bodies. No serif to S.
3	Spode	**c1800-20** Found both with a slight curve, Mark 3, and without, Mark 3a. Occurs on all wares.
3a	Spode	**c1800-20** The more common lower case mark was straight and is found on all wares.

4 SPODE — c1815-33 Used on all bodies up to the end of the Spode period, it may be distinguished from Mark 2 by the serifs on the S. It is frequently found with numbers below it; these are thought to be clay department workmens' marks.

7 SPODES NEW·STONE — 1822-33 Introduced in about 1822 when a new formula was adopted for stone china. Although its use should have ceased in 1833 it may have remained in use to about 1835 or later.

101 COPELAND & GARRETT — 1833-47 Used on all bodies but especially on earthenware and stone china.

204 COPELAND — c1870-1970 Impressed on the white earthenware body called Crown. The exact date of its introduction is not known.

Painted Marks

21 *SPODE.* — c1799-1833 Applied by individual gilders or painters to non-printed wares especially on bone china and stone china. The quality and style of the letters varies greatly.

Printed Marks

31 **Spode** — 1800-20 Commonly found printed in blue on all wares but especially on bone china on which it is often the only mark.

33 S P O D E — 1810-33 The most common printed mark for earthenware and bone china blue prints. Mark 34 occurs on old copper engravings of Buddleia or Trophies-Nankin patterns and may pre-date Mark 33.

33a S P O D E

34 SPODE

36 (SPODE) — 1805-15 A mark rarely seen except on the blue-printed patterns of Buffalo, Rome and Filigree. Introduced about 1805 it possibly remained in use for ten years.

37 SPODE — c1805-18 Rarely found mark on blue-printed wares, but on engraving of Rock pattern has a small version of it, Mark 37a, and the larger Mark 37 occurs on an engraving of Net pattern.

37a SPODE

47 SPODE Stone-China — c1812-33 Believed to be the earliest mark used specifically for Spode's Stone China, it was formed by superimposing Mark 36 upon a pseudo-chinese seal mark. This type of mark was popular among Spode's contemporaries like Miles Mason and William Ridgway.

48 SPODE Stone China — c1814-33 Mark 48 was introduced a short time later possibly to avoid confusion with competitors like Clews who had copied it. Both marks were used concurrently.

132 COPELAND & GARRETT LATE SPODE NEW FAYENCE — 1833-47 Found on earthenware of an ivory colour. In use throughout the period. Usually printed underglaze.

135 COPELAND & GARRETT LATE SPODE — 1833-47 Used throughout the period of the partnership on printed wares and on all bodies.

254 SPODE MANUFACTURERS COPELAND ENGLAND — c1900-10 Printed in green, in use on stone china in 1906. Rare version of an earlier mark to which the word MANUFACTURERS has been added.

258 COPELAND SPODE ENGLAND New Stone — c1920-60 Printed underglaze usually in green even on blue patterns which were transferred onto glost ware and refired in the glost oven to produce an inglaze cobalt blue print.

MARKS		Workmens marks
		Examples found on Patterns
1	/	Willow II, Buffalo, Pearl River House.
2	//	Caramanian, Buffalo, Pearl River House.
3	///	Pearl River House
4	////	Pearl River House
5	⅄	Pearl River House, Buddleia, Buffalo, Forest-Landscape II.
6	⅄⅄	Bridge I, Forest-Landscape II, Tower, Rock.
7	⅄⅄⅄	Mandarin
8	⅄⅄⅄	Various
9	⅃	Buffalo, Blue Italian, Caramanian.
10	o	Various
11	⅄	Flying Pennant, Net.
12	♭	Various

APPENDIX V : CHINESE LANDSCAPE BORDERS

13	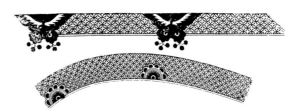	Temple with Panel, Mandarin I, Buffalo.
14		Woodman.
15		Willow I
16		Bridge I, Buffalo
17		Willow III
18		Temple with Panel
19		Net
20		Two Temples II
21		Forest Landscape I, Bridge I
22		Mandarin II
23		Willow I, India, Italian
24		Forest Landscape I
25		Forest Landscape II
26		Caramanian
27		Flower Cross
28		Temple Landscape II, Buddleia

The following designs are used on the borders of Spode's chinese landscape patterns. The name given is either that of the pattern, or of the border, if the border is found on several patterns. For a discussion of the motifs in each border, see the glossary.

Two Figures II Ch. 8, Fig 7.

Two Figures I Spode example not yet seen with this border. Compare Chinese example Ch. 8, Fig 1, and Jug Fig 11.

Buffalo Ch. 11, Fig 9.

Buffalo (not Spode) Ch. 11, Fig 29A.

BUTTERFLY, TRELLIS & KEY BORDERS

Temple-Landscape II (BTK type) Ch. 10, Fig 15.

Temple-Landscape variation Parasol Ch. 10, Fig 18.

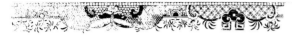

Buddleia (BTK type) Ch. 9, Fig 6.

Forest-Landscape Ch. 9, Figs 11 & 12 and Ch. 6, Fig 16.

Rock I Ch. 6, Fig 16.

Y-WORK BORDERS

Buffalo (non-Spode for comparison) Ch. 11, Fig 32.

BUTTERFLY, HONEYCOMB AND DRAPE BORDERS

Bridge I (BHD type) Ch. 10, Fig 6.

Bridge II (BHD type) Ch. 10, Fig 8.

New Bridge (BHD type) Ch. 10, Fig 10.

Net Ch. 9, Fig 31.

Tall Door Ch. 9, Fig 28.

Flying Pennant Ch. 9, Fig 34.

Willow Pattern III (20th Century engraving) Ch. 5, Fig 8.

Willow Pattern I & II Nankin from early 19th century engraving. Ch. 5, Figs 5 & 7.

TRELLIS DIAPER BORDERS

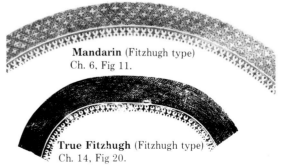

Mandarin (Fitzhugh type) Ch. 6, Fig 11.

True Fitzhugh (Fitzhugh type) Ch. 14, Fig 20.

GLOSSARY

GLOSSARY of terms used in describing the decoration of Chinese landscape patterns.

BAT SYMBOL The bat in China is an emblem of happiness and longevity. The conventional bat is often so ornate that its use in decoration may be confused with the butterfly. Its wings are sometimes curved in the shape of a Joo-I head. A bat symbol occurs in the border of Tall Door pattern. (See Ch. 9, Fig. 28).

BUTTERFLY SYMBOL The butterfly is an emblem of joy, of long life and of summer. It is also a symbol of conjugal felicity. (See Ch. 7, Fig. 3).

Butterflies of different design occur in the borders of Pearl River House (Ch. 8, Fig. 18), Buffalo (Ch. 11, Fig. 9), Temple-Landscape II (Ch. 10, Fig. 15), a Temple-Landscape variation Parasol (Ch. 10, Fig. 18), Two Temples II variation Broseley (Ch. 7, Fig. 16). Buddleia (Ch. 9, Fig. 6), Bridge (Ch. 10, Figs. 8 and 10).

CARTOUCHE This is a white area left so that figures or other features may be shown upon it. It was a device adopted before the skills of engraving had been developed to the point where figures could be shown on a *shaded* background. A good example is seen in Two Figures, which accurately reproduces the same feature in the original Chinese design.

CELL or *Honeycomb* designs. Hexagons, either perfect or irregular, often with radiating lines to the centre of each cell. They may be found as *single cell* beads, as on Buddleia, or as *multi-cell* panels when used in brocade borders. The cells used in this way are often irregular, that is longer one way than the other.

CIRCLET OF PETALS Rather like a necklace consisting of several strings of beads or pearls, this motif occurs on patterns in the Buffalo series. (Ch. 11, Fig. 29A)

CLOUDS The Chinese artist depicted clouds as a series of horizontal coils, as for example in Mandarin pattern.

CLOUD AND WATER The type of decorations called here Chinese Landscapes are sometimes known as Cloud and Water landscapes.

DAGGER or *Spearhead*. The description is traditional, although some examples are depicted more like conventionalised fleur-de-lys. The usual design is interspersed with a second motif, variously described as a *post* or *dumb-bell*. Spode patterns

Lake, Temple with Panel, Mandarin and True Fitzhugh employ this bead below a trellis border.

DIAMOND or *Lozenge* work. A popular design, but more often ornamented in a way that suggests a lattice trellis (q.v.).

DIAPERS are designs which have a square, diamond or other geometric motif repeated to form a uniform interlocking pattern. The word is derived from its use to describe a cloth with such a pattern on it (Greek *diaspros*, *dia*, through, *aspros*, white.)

DRAPE MOTIF occurs on the Bridge II and variation Queen Charlotte clearly reproducing the Chinese designs of the type known in America as Fitzhugh. (Ch. 10, Figs. 6, 8 and 10).

FENCE Seen on many patterns, and always made up of a series of fretted panels which are of the same design except those in Willow Pattern where there are two or three different patterns used, and the fence is more angular than in most other patterns. (Ch. 15, Fig. 4).

FINIAL An ornamental feature terminating the end of the ridge of a tiled roof of a tea house or temple. The two examples which occur on Spode patterns are on the teahouses in Two Figures and Mandarin which illustrate stylised fish tail finials. (Ch. 8, Fig. 7 and Ch. 6, Fig. 11).

FISH ROE Reminiscent of the fish eggs packed closely in fish roe. Two types are found: open packed and close packed.

HUSK CHAIN A simple bead, the best known example occurring on the Chinese service decorated with the insignia of the Society of the Cincinnati.

JOO-I, *or Ju-i, Heads*. The Joo-I is the name of a kind of short sword with a sword guard. The head of the Joo-I, conventionally treated often figures as an ornament.

JUNK A typical junk curves gracefully from a high stern to the bow, with one or more masts supported by rigging. The best example appears in the foreground of Long Bridge pattern. (See Fig. 5).

KEY MOTIF This type of design became popular during the Chou Dynasty and is best seen in the motif used for the standard Willow Pattern. Nearly every border to a Chinese landscape includes a form of this motif.

LOZENGE or *Lattice*. A regular pattern of squares like those on a chequer board. Another use of the term might describe the linked panels in the Two Temples I and Temple-Landscape patterns.

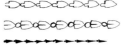

TERMINOLOGY

PAGODA A structure in the form of a many-storeyed *tapering* tower, each storey having a roof which projects less than the one below it. For a typical illustration see Ch. 13, Fig. 14.

PANEL A feature which has a design within a frame. Fences are made up of *fretted* panels, while those on buildings may be solid or of lattice construction. The solid type is seen as the distinguishing feature, for example, of the main building in Temple with Panel. (Ch. 9, Fig. 15).

The other types of panel include the lattice work as seen in the pavilion in Buffalo, or the sides of the house in Long Bridge. (Ch. 11, Fig. 9 and Ch. 12, Fig. 10).

PARASOL A man holding a parasol is a prominent feature of all the Temple-Landscape patterns: they may be of different designs but are all parasols rather than umbrellas and would be carried by men and women.

PAVILION An ornamental building, often with a verandah supported by pillars, and usually of two storeys.

PEDESTAL A structure with tall pillars supporting a roof, as on the island in Temple-Landscape pattern may be a tall grain-burning pedestal.

RECUMBENT SILKWORM C.A.S. Williams illustrates the example of the simple form. The second variety, however, is that which is found on some objects of Buffalo pattern.

ROCKS Depicted as wavy surfaces with shading beneath, rocks are large in area and occur on many patterns.

SAMPAN A vessel for shallow waters often with a simple cabin for sheltering from the sun or rain. Propelled by a pole, examples occur on Two Figures II, Temple-Landscape varieties, and Two Temple varieties.

SCALE WORK An extremely popular form of diaper decoration which was derived from the ornamentation of bronze and other metal objects. Examples of *double scale* are found on Bridge II, and of *Shaded double scale* on Two Temples II varieties.

SCROLLS The scroll is the sacred text of the Buddhist scriptures and the store of truth. Scrolls of this sort feature in the border of Long Bridge pattern.

TEMPLE A building, usually with few, if any, windows intended as a place of religious worship. It may have several storeys, with projecting roofs. (Ch. 5, Fig. 5–7).

TEMPLE GATE The precinct surrounding a temple is sacred and is approached through a Temple gate. An example occurs in Two Temples pattern where the building in the foreground will be a temple gate, with a temple guard in the doorway. (Ch. 7, Fig. 3).

TRELLIS This is a development of the design formed by a structure of crossed bars or laths to form lattice work. The best known example is the border used for True Fitzhugh and Temple with Panel patterns. (Spode pattern 2636 notes it as Nankeen and dagger border).

This design is also known as *lattice work*.

WALLA WALLA A boat with a canopy or a cabin, propelled by a pole. (Ch. 6, Fig. 16).

Y WORK *Open Y-Work*, or Y-diaper is found on Chinese originals and was copied by Spode in his reproduction of Rock I, and the engraving in Chapter 6, Fig. 19 is a good example.

False Y-work is the name given to the pattern of triangles used by an unknown manufacturer for the border of a Buffalo pattern. (Ch. 11, Fig. 32).

AQUA FORTIS The impure fuming nitric acid of commerce.

ARGYLL A vessel for keeping gravy warm; similar in shape to a coffee pot, it has an inner compartment into which hot water is poured.

BACKSTONE The flat round iron plate on which the transfer-printer keeps the colour warm on the stove; a colloquial spelling of 'bakestone', a similar plate on which cakes were baked.

BALSAM CAPIVI Like Balsam of Sulphur (sulphurated oil)which is a mixture of flowers of sulphur and olive oil; it was used to cause the colour to float on the copper plate and the paper to float off in the water.

BARYTES Naturally occuring Barium Sulphate, Ba SO₄.

BAT (1) A tile or slab of refractory material used to support pottery ware while it is being fired. (2) A flat slab of plaster used for supporting clay ware until it is fired. (3) A disc of clay flattened by hand or machine prior to shaping. (4) A sheet of glue used in bat printing. Almost anything flat.

BISCUIT See Firing.

BITSTONE Calcined flint or broken pitchers (q.v.), in either case crushed to about ⅛ inch (4 mm) scattered in the bottom of a saggar to prevent ware sticking during the glost firing.

BLACK FLUX Used for smelting metallic ores, it exercised a reducing action and promoted fusion. The product consists of potassium carbonate mixed with charcoal.

BLUE CALX The black oxide of cobalt, CoO. Probably a slightly impure form in the days when this term was used.

BONE CHINA A hard, vitreous ceramic body renowned for its strength, whiteness and translucency and the richness of enamel on-glaze colours obtainable. The usual composition is: calcined cattle bone 45-50%, china clay 20-25%, Cornish or china stone 25-30%. Clayware fired to biscuit stage at 1200-1250° (2192-2282°F), glazed and refired at 1050-1100°C (1922-2012°F). Developed by Josiah Spode I in the 1790's and marketed after his death in 1797 by his son, Josiah Spode II in about 1799.

BORAX Commercial Sodium bi-borate, $2NaBO^2 B^2 O^3$. Native sodium borate was known as Tincal. When heated it melts to a clear glass.

BOTTLE OVEN The old coal-fired intermittent kilns protected by a bottle-shaped hovel which increased the draught and enabled the fireman to control the firing process.

BUNG A column or pile of saggars. Similarly a pile of flatware, as a 'bung of plates'.

CADOGAN TEAPOT A design based on a Chinese wine-pot without a lid, it was adapted in England for serving tea. First made at the Rockingham Factory at Swinton, Yorkshire c. 1795, it was usually made in a glazed redware. Also made by Spode, Copeland & Garrett, Davenport and others.

CALCINE To roast a solid substance to expel its more volatile parts or to change its nature, e.g. increase its friability.

CALKING Alternative term for calcining.

CALX The residual mass of any metal that has been subjected to strong heat in the presence of air, i.e. calcined. The calces are generally equivalent to what the modern chemist calls 'metallic oxides'.

CHINA PITCHERS Broken pieces of china which have been fired to biscuit temperature but not glost. Pulverised for use in colours as an inert filler.

CHINAWARE The term used to describe the true porcelain wares exported from China through the ports of Canton and Macao. Known today as Chinese Export Porcelain, China Trade Porcelain, *Porcelaine des Indes*, or Oriental Lowestoft.

CLOBBERED WARE A design produced in underglaze blue – often chinese – to which enamel painting has been added. Designs printed with outlines for intentional painting in with either under- or on-glaze colours are not considered to be clobbered ware but printed and painted.

CORNISH STONE or CHINA STONE Partly decomposed granite consisting of feldspathic minerals and quartz. Equivalent to the chinese *petuntze*, it is used as a flux in ceramic bodies and glazes. Cornish stone was available in various grades, e.g. Hard Purple (the most fusible), Mild Purple, Hard White, and Dry or Soft White (the least fusible and only slightly less decomposed than china clay). The purple stones owe their coloration to the presence of a small amount of fluorspar.

CRANK A refractory structure for supporting flatware during the glost and decorating firings.

CREAMWARE Or cream-coloured earthenware, was introduced about 1740. It was made by applying a lead glaze to a body similar to that in use for coloured glazes and salt-glazed stoneware. It was later greatly improved by Josiah Wedgwood I who named his product 'Queensware'.

CUPEL A small refractory vessel used in the assay of precious and other non-ferrous metal ores. Shaped like a tapered cylinder, broad end up, with a shallow depression in the top, cupels are made of bone-ash or calcined magnesia.

DECORATING FIRING The heat treatment of pottery-ware after the application of coloured or metallic (*e.g.* gilded) decoration. The temperature, usually 700-800°C (1292-1472°F), fixes the decoration and ensures its durability. See Firing.

DELFTWARE See Tin-glazed earthenware.

EARTHENWARE A ceramic ware made from clays and silica compounds, which, when fired, is porous and opaque. It is usually glazed to render it impervious to liquids. Firing temperatures today are, for biscuit 1100-1150°C (2012-2100°F), and for glost 1060-1100°C (1940-2012°F). Compositions today are based on Ball clay 25%, China clay 25%, Flint 35%, Cornish stone 15%. Quartz sand may be substituted for flint and Felspar for the stone. Earthenwares of the first half of the eighteenth century were of flint and ball or pipe clay only.

ENAMEL FIRING See Decorating firing.

FIRING The process of heat treatment of ceramic wares. (1)

Approximate firing temperatures

	°C	°F
Biscuit		
Bone china	1200-1250	2192-2282
Porcelain	900-1000	1652-1832
Earthenware	1100-1150	2012-2100
Stone china	1140	2084
Glost		
Bone china	1050-1100	1922-2012
Porcelain	1350-1400	2462-2552
Earthenware	1060-1100	1940-2012
Decorating		
Cobalt colours	1000-1100	1832-2012
Hardening on	600-760	1112-1400
Ground-laid colours	820-900	1508-1652
Enamel colours	700-800	1292-1472
Gold or Platinum	720-750	1328-1382

When clayware is fired it is transformed into a hard substance by irreversible reactions. This condition is called 'biscuit'. (2) After the glaze has been applied to the biscuit ware the pieces are placed and fired in the 'glost' oven. It is then known as 'glost' ware, or white ware or white glost. (3) Decoration added over the glaze needs to be fired at temperatures below about 950°C (1742°F). (4) Transfer prints and painted decoration applied to the biscuit, or over the glaze for firing 'in-glaze' will need to withstand the glost firing temperature.

FLINT Almost pure silica, SiO_2, was originally collected from the beaches of the English Channel and North Sea. In the period 1715-20 flint began to replace sand in earthenware bodies when whiteness was required. It has to be calcined to render it easy to grind. It was the principal source of silica in ceramic recipes until recently.

FLINTED SAGGARS Newly fired saggars for glostware that have had the inside surfaces washed over with a well-stirred mixture of flint and clay in water. This renders the surface less porous and so reduces the amount of glaze absorbed from the dipped ware when this glaze reaches the point of volatilization.

FLINT GLASS Colourless glass containing lead oxide and silica which was introduced into the batch of ingredients for a colour.

FLUX A material which lowers the temperature at which a mixture of ceramic substances melts.

FOREBUNG In a bottle-oven the last bung of saggars to be set in before the oven entrance ('clammins') was sealed. A high temperature could be achieved because the top of this bung was directly above the flames.

FRIT A glassy material produced by fusing a mixture of some or all of the ingredients of a glaze, quenching and pulverizing them. The purpose is to render insoluble any soluble or toxic materials present and to drive off gases which might disturb the surface appearance of the glaze later. It is also to ensure greater homogeneity in the glaze so that the melting point is lowered in the glost fire. The process ensures that lead compounds are made safe.

Frit, verb, to fuse partially.

GLOST See Firing

GRAY PAPER Circular, cut, unsized coarse-textured paper used for filtering liquids through a funnel. This paper contained wool as well as jute and esparto grass, all in an unbleached state.

HARDENING ON The firing of decorations applied by transfer printing direct to the biscuit ware. It fixes the colour to the ware and volatilizes the printing oils.

HONG MERCHANT The Chinese merchant made responsible by the Chinese government for supervising the trading activities with the East India Companies in Canton. A Hong was a factory, i.e. the warehouse of a factory as opposed to a manufactory, on the banks of the Pearl River at Canton owned by one of the East India Companies and used as a depot for the storage of goods, both imported and awaiting shipment.

HOVEL The conical building surrounding a kiln or oven.

HUMPER An object in which the centre has become domed during firing. A manufacturing fault usually due to incorrect placing of the clay ware.

INDIA CHINA A term, seldom-used, for stone china. Chinese porcelain for the West was imported in ships of the East India Companies and China trade was often included as part of the 'trade with the Indies'. This chinese porcelain was sometimes called India china.

IRONSTONE The name 'Ironstone China' was adopted by C.J. Mason in 1813 (Patent No. 3724) to describe a ware made to a formula similar, if not identical, to stone china. The formula quoted in the patent must be regarded as spurious, because it included about 25% iron slag. By the 1840's the term had been debased to describe the medium to lower qualities of earthenware. Today, the term is equivalent to earthenware.

LEAD: RED LEAD Red oxide of lead, Pb_3O_4 is added to printing oil to throw up the greasy scum while boiling so that it may be 'fired away', that is ignited and burnt as it rises to the surface. It also helps to fix the oil and colour onto the ware. WHITE LEAD Lead carbonate, $2PbCO_3 Pb(OH)_2$. Performs a similar function to red lead.

Both forms of lead were used in glazes before the introduction of lead bisilicate, but much of the raw lead was fritted first.

LIME CaO, was added as Whiting to some ceramic bodies, glazes and colours.

LINSEED OIL See Oils.

LITHARGE Lead monoxide, PbO, was used for the same purpose as red lead, but was generally preferred in oils for printing *on* the glaze.

LYNN SAND Is almost pure silica and so is selected for use in the manufacture of ceramics.

MAGNESIA Magnesium oxide, MgO, is a basic oxide and very refractory.

MARINE ACID Hydrochloric acid.

MATCHING A trade term to describe a replacement of a design made earlier·either by the same or a different manufacturer. The Spode factory made many matchings of wares from China, also some of Chelsea and Worcester porcelains.

MUFFLE A furnace or kiln in which there is a compartment where ceramic objects or substances (e.g. colours) can be heated free from contact with the fuel and its products of combustion.

NITRE Potassium nitrate, KNO_3.

OIL OF AMBER Is made from coarse pieces of amber distilled in an iron retort. The oil is separated from the liquor and succinic acid, and rectified with six times its volume of water. It was used as a drying oil, to prevent the colour rubbing off the ware.

OIL: LINSEED OIL From the seed of the common flax, it is the base of printing oils. It should be of good quality and old.

OIL: RAPE OIL From the Brassica napus, a plant like the turnip. Used in printing oil because it is softer than linseed oil and when added helps it to work better, as well as assisting the paper to wash off the ware.

OLD GOLD A yellow colour applied to the edge of an object, usually earthenware, to give the semblance of a gilded edge.

PATTERN NUMBERS Spode pattern books date from about 1800, but only those patterns which were decorated on the glaze and required an enamel decorating firing were so recorded until about 1822, when patterns coloured underglaze were also recorded as B numbers. About 150 pattern numbers were recorded each year during the Spode period from 1800–1834.

Approximate dates of Spode Patterns

1800–01	1– 150	1812–13	–1950	1824–25	–3750
–02	– 300	–14	–2100	–26	–3900
–03	– 450	–15	–2250	–27	–4050
–04	– 600	–16	–2400	–28	–4200
–05	– 750	–17	–2550	–29	–4350
–06	– 900	–18	–2700	–30	–4500
–07	–1050	–19	–2850	–31	–4650
–08	–1200	–20	–3000	–32	–4800
–09	–1350	–21	–3150	–33	–4950
–10	–1500	–22	–3300	–34	–5100
–11	–1650	–23	–3450		
–12	–1800	–24	–3600		

PEARL ASH Potassium carbonate, K_2CO_3, used in glazes and colours.

PEARLWARE White earthenware, similar to early creamware, but with some cobalt added to the lead glaze to impart a white appearance. Used almost exclusively for underglaze transfer-printed ware.

'PINK' HEIGHT A medium temperature in the glost oven. Underglaze pink colours were placed low down in the second and third rings of saggars where the temperature would have been about 1000°C (1832°F).

PITCHERS Pottery which has been broken in the course of manufacture. Biscuit pitchers are crushed and ground for use as inert fillers or as Bitstone (qv.).

PLASTER Plaster of Paris, calcium sulphate, $(CaSO_4)_2 H_2O$. So called because of the large deposits of gypsum used for the manufacture of plaster at Montmartre, Paris.

PLATE

The following terms describe the different features of a plate.

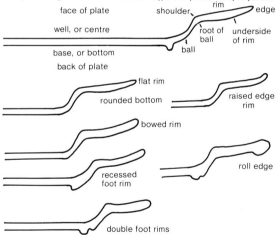

rim The outermost flattish part of a plate or dish.

edge The outer extremity of a piece, on which it is customary to apply a line of colour or gold, as in a gilded edge.

shoulder The point at which the contour of the face of a plate or dish steepens downwards, away from the rim towards the centre.

centre, or well When applied to an object, the centre is the middle, flat part of it. When applied to a decoration, it is that part of the design which occupies the principal area (a piece, as opposed to the border.

PORCELAIN A vitreous, translucent ceramic usually pale grey in colour. Invented in China during the tenth century AD, this ceramic body is known as true porcelain, or hard paste: it is made of kao-lin, (china clay) and petuntze (cornish stone) in about equal proportions.

In 1709 J.F. Böttger at Meissen discovered the secret of this porcelain formula. Elsewhere in Europe artificial, or soft paste, porcelains using glassy frits had been developed. The famous English potteries of Chelsea, Bow, Worcester, Derby, Lowestoft, Longton Hall and others made artificial porcelain.

William Cookworthy discovered the essential ingredients china clay and cornish stone in 1747 and, using these, patented a formula and process in 1768. This was renewed by Act of Parliament in 1775 by Richard Champion who sold the rights to a consortium of potters in Hanley which became the New Hall China Manufactory.

True porcelain clayware is fired at a low temperature, 900°C (1652°F), then at 1400°C (2552°F) for glost. It can also be fired once only. Artificial porcelain is less refractory, being fired at about 1200°C (2192°F) biscuit, dipped in a lead glaze and glost fired at about 1050°C (1922°F). It may also be called fritted porcelain.

POTASH Potassium carbonate, K_2CO_3.

QUEENSWARE An improved form of cream coloured earthenware perfected by Josiah Wedgwood in 1762.

REVERBERATORY FURNACE One in which the flame is turned back over the substance to be heated.

SAGGAR A box or container made of fireclay and grog (crushed fired saggars or pitchers) in which pottery ware may be placed for setting in a kiln. The saggar protects the ware from the flames and kiln gases. By placing the saggars one upon another in bungs, or tall columns, it was possible to load a bottle oven with thousands of pieces of pottery.

Kiln furniture: see Chapter 3

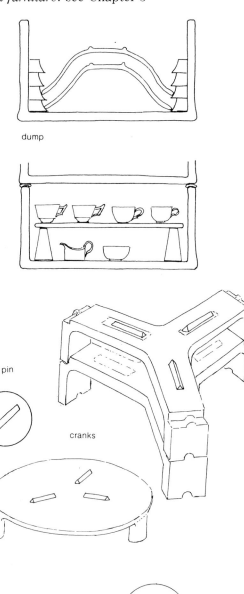

dump

pin

cranks

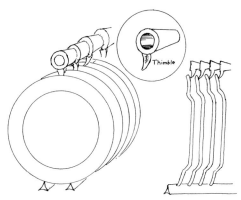

Thimble

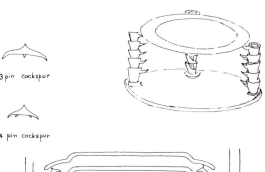

3 pin cockspur

4 pin cockspur

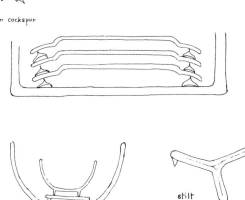

stilt

SALT GLAZED STONEWARE See Stoneware.

SAND BATH A vessel containing sand on which a flask or beaker containing the substance might rest above a source of heat so that direct exposure to that heat source is avoided.

SCORIA Dross or slag from the smelting of metal.

SIZE A solution used to treat the surface of pottery ware or materials used in its manufacture.

Printer's size: a fluid mixture of soft soap and water brushed onto the tissue paper.

Engraver's size: a mixture of turpentine and resin for rendering the surface of a copper plate able to accept a traced pencil line.

SLAG The semi-vitrified compounds produced during the reduction of metallic ores by fluxes.

SLIPPED WARE Porous earthenware of a dark body to which has been applied a coating of clay slip (mixture of clay materials in water), or engobe, to change the colour of the ware of parts of it.

SODA Sodium monoxide, Na_2O.

SODA ASH Anhydrous sodium carbonate, Na_2CO_3.

SPIRITS OF TAR A liquid bitumen prepared from the wood of pine and other trees by heat.

SPUR The triangular support used to separate plates in firing.

STONE CHINA A type of fine, pale grey porcelainous stoneware, hard, dense and sometimes translucent. Developed by John and William Turner of Lane End, Stoke-on-Trent, in 1800 it was known as 'Turner's Patent',(Patent No. 2367). Spode II and Miles Mason re-introduced it in about 1812.

No link has been found, so far, between the Turner patent and Spode's manufacture. The previously suggested date of 1805 for its introduction by Spode has been discussed by L. Whiter in his book *Spode*, pp. 188–192.

STONEWARE, WHITE SALT-GLAZED A white or cream coloured body when fired with a semi-shiny glaze. Glazed by throwing salt into the oven when the temperature had reached about 1200° (2192°F) at which the sodium and chlorine separate to allow the sodium to combine with the silica on the surface of the red hot clayware to form a sodium silicate glaze which makes the ware vitreous.

TAR Was used to cause the colour to flow and the paper to float off easily; it also opens the oil and enables the other ingredients to go further. Barbadoes tar or asphalt was purer and was generally used in oils for printing on the glaze.

TARTAR Impure bitartrate of potassium.

TEA HOUSE The tea ceremony has distinctly religious connections and special houses are built for the purpose of celebrating this ceremony. It is possible that many of the buildings which feature prominently in Chinese landscape designs are really tea houses rather than temples or mandarin's houses. The main building in Two Figures pattern is probably a tea house, as is that in Mandarin.

TINCAL Native sodium borate from which borax is obtained.

TIN-GLAZED EARTHENWARE A porous bodied earthenware with a lead glaze made opaque by the addition of tin oxide. Also known as Delft ware, but the process was in use in England in the 16th century.

TONNY 'fashionable': This term could be the adjectival form of the Regency word 'ton', meaning the vogue, mode or in fashion. Thus a 'tonny oriental' might refer to some fashionable oriental design.

TRENCHER SALT A salt cellar without feet, and with a depression in the centre. It may be round, oval or rectangular.

VITREOUS The state of a ceramic body which has been rendered non-porous by firing without the addition of a glaze.

WHIRLER An object of flatware (plate, saucer or platter) in which the centre has fallen below the level of the foot rim. A manufacturing fault causing the object to wobble or whirl.

WHITEWARE Usually undecorated glost ware. Also used to refer to white-bodied earthenware decorated or undecorated, and white saltglazed stoneware of the eighteenth century. See also Firing.

WHITING Finely ground chalk, $CaCO_3$. It is used as a source of lime in ceramic bodies, glazes and colours.

WIND FURNACE One into which air is forced so that the heat may be more intense.

REFERENCES and BIBLIOGRAPHY

Acts of Parliament. See Footnotes to Chapter 1

1. 15 GeoIII Cap 52 (1775) An Act for enlarging the Term of Letters Patent granted by His Majesty to William Cookworthy of Plymouth, etc.

2. ALLAN, J.W. (1973). *Abu'l–Qasim's Treatise on Ceramics.* Jnl. Persian Studies. Iran **XI**. p. 112

3. *Ibid* p. 116

4. *Ibid* p. 120

ANDREWS, R.W. (1962) *Cobalt.* Overseas Geological Survey: Mineral Resources Division. London: H.M.S.O.

5. Anon. (1960) *Cobalt Monograph.* Brussels: Centre d'Information du Cobalt p. 1 (cites Brown, T.B. (1948) *Excavations in Azerbaijan*)

6. *Ibid* p. 2 (cites Berg, G. and Friedensburg, F. (1944) *Die Metallischen Rohstoffe*, Vol. VI: Nickel und Kobalt. Stuttgart: F. Enke Verlag. p. 210)

7. *Ibid* p. 127–8

8. *Ibid* p. 441

9. Anon. (1956) *Facsimile of George Washington Original Cincinnati Dinner Plate 1785.* Boston: Massachusetts Society of the Cincinnati. 1955.

10. Anon. (1819) *Catalogue of the sale of the Collection of HM Queen Charlotte by Mr Christie.* See footnote to Chapter 10.

11. Anon (1936) *Materials and Processes of the Ceramic Industries – Decoration.* Monthly Bulletin for the Ceramic Industry, Stoke-on-Trent: C.E. Ramsden & Co. Ltd. No. **95** Jan 1936.

12. Anon. (1950) *Cobalt in the Ceramic Industries.* Nos. **152** and **153**. June and July 1950.

BARRETT, F.A. (1951) *Caughley and Coalport Porcelain*, Leigh-on-Sea: Lewis.

13. BARSTOW, R. (1971) Personal communication to the author.

14. BARTON, R.M. (1966) *A History of the Cornish China Clay Industry.* p. 25. Truro: Bradford Barton.

BAUER, J. (1974) *A Field Guide to Minerals, Rocks and Precious Stones.* p. 180. London: Octopus 1975 (reprint)

15. BELL, R.C. (1971) *Tyneside Pottery.* p. 130. London: Studio Vista.

16. BELLAIGUE, G. de (1976) Personal communication to the author.

BEURDELEY, M. (1962) *Porcelain of the East India Companies.* London: Barrie and Rockcliff.

BILBREY, J.H. (   ) *Cobalt. A Materials Survey.* Information Circular 8103 U.S. Bureau of Mines.

17. BRANKSTON, A.D. (1938) *Early Ming wares of Ching-të Chên.* P. 16. Peking: Henri Vetch.

18. *Ibid* p. 102.

19. *Ibid* pl. 26d.

20. BRUCHMUELLER, W. (1897) Der Kobaltbergbau und die Blaufarbenwerke in Sachsen bis Zum Jahre 1653. Translation by G.R. Mickle in the *Early History of the Cobalt Industry in Saxony*: Ontario Bureau of Mines Annual Report for 1913, XIX, Part II, Appendix III, p. 235

21. *Ibid* p. 237

22. CARTER, G. (1964) *Outlines of English History from 55 BC to AD 1963.* p. 106–113. London: Ward Lock.

23. CARTWRIGHT, C. (1788) *Orders and Regulations of the East India Company.*

24. CASTRO, J.P. de (1926) *The Law and Practice of Hallmarking Gold and Silver Wares*, p. 54–56. London: Crosby Lockwood. See also Appendix to Chapter I.

25. CHAFFERS, W. (1932 ed) *Marks and Monograms on European and Oriental Pottery and Porcelain* with historical notices of each Manufactory. (Ed. F. Litchfield) p. 767. London: Reeves and Turner, Fourteenth edition.

26. CHAMBERLAIN, W. (1977) *The Thames and Hudson Manual of Etching and Engraving.* p. 115 et seq. London: Thames and Hudson.

CHARLES, B.H. (1974) *Pottery and Porcelain. A Glossary of Terms.* Newton Abbot: David and Charles.

27. CHARLESTON R.J. & WATNEY, B. (1966) Petitions for Patents concerning Porcelain, Glass and Enamels, with special reference to Birmingham, 'The Great Toyshop of Europe'. *Trans. Eng. Cer. Cir.* **6** pt 2, p. 66–67.

28. *Ibid* p. 80.

29. COLLARD, E. (1967) *Nineteenth-Century Pottery and Porcelain in Canada.* pl. 33B. Montreal: McGill University Press.

30. COOLEY, A.J. (1880) *Cooley's Cyclopaedia of Practical Receipts* and collateral information in the Arts, Manufactures, Professions and Trades. Sixth edition. London: Churchill.

31. COPELAND R. (1967) Josiah Spode and the Chinese Trade. *Canadian Antiques Collector.* Toronto. p. 15–18.

32. COPELAND, R. (1972) *A Short History of Pottery Raw Materials and the Cheddleton Flint Mill.* Leek, Staffordshire.

33. COPELAND, R. (1977) Josiah Spode and the China Trade. *Trans. Eng. Cer. Cir.* **10** Pt 2, p. 99–108.

34. COYSH, A.W. (1970) *Blue and White Transfer Ware 1780–1840.* p. 10 Newton Abbott: David and Charles. Referred to in text as Coysh I.

35. *Ibid* p. 16.

36. *Ibid* p. 18.

37. *Ibid* p. 24.

38. *Ibid* p. 66.

39. *Ibid* p. 96.

40. COYSH, A.W. (1972) *Blue Printed Earthenware 1800–1850.* p. 22. Newton Abbott: David & Charles. Referred to in text as Coysh II.

41. *Ibid* p. 30.

42. *Ibid* p. 68.

43. *Ibid* p. 98.

DANIELL, T & W. (1810) *Picturesque Voyage to India by Way of China.*

44. EVANS, W. (1846) *The Art and History of the Potting Business.* Shelton, Stoke-on-Trent.

45. FINER, A & SAVAGE, G. ed (1965) *The Selected Letters of Josiah Wedgwood.* p. 8. London: Cory, Adams & Mackay.

46. *Ibid.* p. 9.

47. FONTAINES, J.K. des (1961) Staffordshire Under-glaze Blue Printed Earthenware of the Early Nineteenth-Century. *Proceedings of the Wedgwood Society.* London. 4, p. 225–231.

48. FONTAINES, J.K. des (1969) Underglaze Blue-printed Earthenware with Particular Reference to Spode. *Trans. Engl. Cer. Cir.* **7**. Part 2, p. 120 et seq.

49. FONTAINES, U. des (1975) Early Printed Patterns at Etruria. *Proceedings of the Wedgwood Society.* London: **9**. p. 10.

50. *Ibid.* pp. 12–13 cites Wedgwood Archives 18.16510.

51. FORBES, H.A.C. (1978) Personal communication to the author.

52. FORREST, D. (1973) *Tea for the British*. The Social and Economic History of a Famous Trade. p. 23. London: Chatto & Windus.

53. *Ibid.* p. 68.

54. *Ibid.* p. 73.

55. *Ibid.* p. 74.

56. *Ibid.* pp. 284–5, Appendix II – citing records of Tea sales, and HM Customs and Excise records of Imports. Despite the reimposition of heavy taxes on tea, which rose to 90% in 1806, the table shows that imports remained steady for over twenty years.

57. FURNIVAL, W.J. (1904) *Leadless Decorative Tiles, Faience and Mosaic*. pp. 385–391. Stone: Staffordshire: W.J. Furnival.

58. GARNER, H. (1954) *Oriental Blue and White*. p. 15. London: Faber & Faber.

59. GODDEN, G. (1968) *Minton Pottery & Porcelain of the First Period, 1793–1850*. p. 1. London: Herbert Jenkins.

60. *Ibid.* pp. 141–149.

61. GODDEN, G.A. (1969) *Caughley & Worcester Porcelain 1775–1800*. p. 10. London: Herbert Jenkins.

62. *Ibid.* p. 16.

63. *Ibid.* p. 17.

64. *Ibid.* p. 18.

65. *Ibid.* p. 21.

66. *Ibid.* p. 23.

67. *Ibid.* p. 117.

68. GODDEN, G.A. (1970) *Coalport & Coalbrookdale Porcelains*. p. 29. London: Herbert Jenkins.

69. GODDEN, G.A. (1972) The Willow Pattern. *The Antique Collector*, June 1972. pp. 148–150.

70. GODDEN, G.A. (1974) *British Pottery – An Illustrated Guide*. p. 235. London: Barrie & Jenkins.

71. *Ibid.* p. 236.

72. *Ibid.* p. 240

73. GODDEN, G. (1974) *An Introduction to English Blue and White Porcelains*. p. 27. Worthing.

74. *Ibid.* p. 47.

75. *Ibid.* p. 49.

76. GORDON, E. (1978) *Collecting Chinese Export Porcelain*. p. 119. London: John Murray.

77. GRANT-DAVIDSON, W.J. (1967) Excavations at Caughley. Trans. Eng. Cer. Cir. **6**, Pt. 3. pp. 272–3.

GRIFFIN, A. (1978) *The Copper plate method of Ceramic Transfer Making* with special reference to Spode Limited, North Staffordshire Polytechnic: Unpublished project for Degree course.

78. HAGGAR, R.G. (1952) *The Masons of Lane Delph and the Origins of Mason's Patent Ironstone China*. p. 26, plates 7, 11 and 12. London: Lund Humphries.

79. HAGGAR, R.G. (1973) Abner Wedgwood's Recipe Book. *Jnl. Northern Ceramic Society*. **I**. p. 30.

80. HAGGAR, R.G. (1975) Black-Printing on Porcelain. *Trans. Eng. Cer. Cir.* **10**. Pt. 1 (1976) pp. 39–53.

81. HAGGAR, R. & ADAMS, E. (1977) *Mason Porcelain and Ironstone 1796–1853*. Miles Mason and the Mason Manufactories. London: Faber & Faber.

82. HAGGAR R. & MANKOWITZ, W. (1957) *The Concise Encyclopedia of English Pottery and Porcelain*. p. 66. London: André Deutsch.

83. *Ibid.* p. 119.

84. *Ibid.* p. 208.

85. HANCOCK, E. (1962) *Chinese and English Decorated Ceramics 1600–1850 A.D.*, Exhibition catalogue, Herbert Art Gallery and Museum, Coventry.

86. HAYDEN, A. (1925) *Spode and His Successors*. p. 194. London: Cassell.

87. *Ibid.* p. 331.

88. HEAL, A. (1925) *London Tradesmen's Cards of the XVIII Century*. An account of their origin and use. Plate xxi. London: Batsford.

89. HILLIER, B. (1965) *The Turners of Lane End: Master Potters of the Industrial Revolution*. p. 73. London: Cory, Adams & Mackay.

90. HOLGATE, D. (1971) *New Hall and its Imitators*. p. 57. London: Faber & Faber.

91. HOLMES, J.B.S. (1966) Fitzhugh and FitzHughs in the China Trade. *Antiques* Magazine: Jan. 1966. pp. 130–131.

92. HOWARD, D.S. (1974) *Chinese Armorial Porcelain*. p. 501. London: Faber & Faber.

93. *Ibid.* pp. 53–55.

94. *Ibid.* p. 587.

95. *Ibid.* p. 602.

96. *Ibid.* p. 691.

97. HOWARD, D.S. & AYERS, J. (1978) *China for the West*. Chinese Porcelain and other decorative arts for export, illustrated from the Mottahedeh Collection. p. 179. London: Sotheby Parke Bernet Publications.

98. *Ibid.* pp. 546–547.

99. HUGHES, B. & T. (1955) *English Porcelain and Bone China, 1743–1850*. pp. 30–36. London: Lutterworth.

100. *Ibid.* p. 80.

101. HUGHES, G.B. (1954) The Development of Cobalt Blue. *Country Life*. **CXV** (June 3). pp. 1824–27.

102. HUME, I.N. (1969) *Pottery and Porcelain in Colonial Williamsburg's Archaeological Collections*. p. 24.

103. HUME, I.N. (1972) Creamware to Pearlware: a Williamsburg perspective. *Ceramics in America*. Ed. IMG Quimby. Winterthur Conference Report 1972. Winterthur: The Henry Francis du Pont Winterthur Museum. p. 247.

104. HUNSTADBRATEN, K. (1971–76) Personal correspondence. Modum, Norway, where there was once an important cobalt mine.)

105. HYDE, J.A. LLOYD (1954) *Oriental Lowestoft, Chinese Export Porcelain*, Porcelaine de la Cie des Indes, p. 110. Newport: Monmouthshire: The Ceramic Book Company. (2nd Ed.).

India Office Records. See Chapter 1 Appendix.

106. JENYNS, S. (1951) *Later Chinese Porcelain: the Ch'ing Dynasty, 1644–1922.* p. 41. London: Faber & Faber. Cites Bushell, S.W. (1899) Oriental Ceramic Art. p. 438.

107. JEWITT, L. (1883) *The Ceramic Art of Great Britain*. p. 396 (Second Edition). London: J.S. Virtue.

108. JONES, E.S. (1955) The Willow Pattern: new legends for old. *Antiques*: **LXVII**. No. 1 January 1955. New York. pp. 50–52.

109. JOURDAIN M. & JENYNS R.S. (1950) Chinese Export Art in the Eighteenth Century. p. 42. London: *Country Life*.

110. KEELE UNIVERSITY LIBRARY. Temporary Ref. (1978) Mosley 337.

111. Spode MSS 926.

112. KEYES, H.E. (1930) The Cincinnati and Their Porcelain. *Antiques* Magazine: **XVII** Feb. 1930. pp. 132–136. Homer Eaton Keyes quotes a letter written from Mount Vernon, Washington's home, under date of August 17, 1785, to Colonel Tilghman: 'If great bargains are to be had, I would supply myself agreeably to an enclosed list.' The cargo of the Pallas contained among many other goods 'Table sets of the best Nankin blue and white Stone China...'. All the porcelain in this list was described as Stone China. (p. 135).

113. LAWRENCE, H. (1974) Wedgwood & Co. *The Connoisseur* **186**. No. 748, pp. 110-116.

114. LEHMANN, I.H. (1969) Kobaltchronologie. Technische Mitteilungen, **10**. Translated by P.G. Smyrk. (1976).

115. LITTLE, W.L. (1969) *Staffordshire Blue* – Underglaze blue transfer-printed earthenware. London: Batsford. Illustrates a plate   , plate 75.

116. LOCKETT, T.A. (1972) *Davenport Pottery and Porcelain, 1794-1887*. p. 48. Newton Abbot: David & Charles.

117. *Ibid*. p. 60.

118. *Ibid*. p. 62. LUEDDERS, A.R. Ed. (1977) *Wedgwood: its Competitors & Imitators, 1800–1830*. Michigan: Ars Ceramica for Wedgwood International Seminar, (May 1977, Dearborn).

119. MCNALLY, S.J. (1976–78) Personal communication. See Appendix and Notes to Chapter 1.

120. MALLET, F. (1973) An Unrecorded Spode Print. *The Connoisseur* September 1973. pp. 23–27.

121. MELLOR, J.W. (1935) *A Comprehensive Treatise on Inorganic and Theoretical Chemistry*. Vol. XIV, p. 424. London: Longmans, Green.

122 *Ibid*. p. 159.

123. METEYARD, E. (1865) *The Life and Works of Josiah Wedgwood*. Vol. 1, p. 357. London: Hurst & Blackett.

124. MINTON MSS 1228.

125. MACINTOSH, D. (1977) *Chinese Blue & White Porcelain*. Newton Abbott: David & Charles.

126. MORSE, H.B. (1929) *The East India Company Trade to China, 1635–1834* **2** Appendix. Oxford: Clarendon Press. See Notes to Chapter 1.

127. *Ibid*. **5**. p. 87.

128. *Ibid*. p. 137.

129. *Ibid*. p. 157.

130. *Ibid*. pp. 168–169.

131. NANCE, E.M. (1942) *The Pottery and Porcelain of Swansea & Nantgarw*. pp. 50–51. London: Batsford.

132. NICHOLLS, R. (1932) *Ten Generations of a Potting Family*. p. 86. London: Lund, Humphries.

133. PALMER, A.M. (1976) *A Winterthur Guide to Chinese Export Porcelain*. p. 133. New York: Crown Publishers Inc.

134. PARKINSON, C.N. (1937) *Trade in the Eastern Seas, 1793–1813*. Cambridge. Cited by S.H. Twining (q.v.).

135. PHILLIPS, J.G. (1956) *China-Trade Porcelain*. An account of its historical background, manufacture, and decoration and a Study of the Helena Woolworth McCann Collection. p. 7. Cambridge, Massachusetts: Harvard University Press; London distributor: Phaidon Press.

136. PROUDLOVE, H. (1969) *The Impact of Tea on the Manufacture of China*, with particular reference to Spode, 1750–1850. Unpublished paper. Cites – India Office Records, Home Miscellaneous, p. 120.

137. REES, A. (1819-1820) The Cyclopaedia; or Universal Dictionary of the Arts, Sciences and Literature, known as 'Rees's Manufacturing Industry'. **IV**. p. 206. Newton Abbot: David & Charles. Reprints (1972).

138. RICHARDSON, W. (1780) A pamphlet first printed in 1779. Advice to the Unwary: or an abstract of certain penal laws now in force, against smuggling in general, and the adulteration of tea;... India Office Records, Home Miscellaneous Series, Vol. 497, pp. 259–291.

139. RICHARDSON, W. (1783) A Plan to prevent Smuggling Tea, by taking off all the present Duties of Customs and Excise on Tea and laying a Small Tax on such Houses only as pay the Window Tax, by which means the Kingdom at large would be greatly benefitted. India Office Records, Home Miscellaneous Series, Vol 61, pp. 139–155.

140. ROBERTS, CLIFTON (1919) Salopian China. Three articles in *The Connoisseur*. **LIV** August 1919 pp. 187–194; December 1919, pp. 223–232; July 1920, pp. 143–153.

141. ROBINSON, F.P. (1912) *The Trade of the East India Company from 1709–1813*. p. 108. Cambridge.

142. *Ibid*. p. 110.

143. *Ibid*. p. 128.

144. ROTH, R. (1961) *Tea Drinking in 18th Century America; Its Etiquette and Equipage*. p. 64. United States National Museum Bulletin 225. Contributions from the Museum of History and Technology, Paper 14. Washington DC: Smithsonian Institution.

145. RUSHMAN, D.F. & CORK, W.B. (1976) Personal Communication. Reckitts (Colours) Limited.

146. SANDON, H. (1969) *The Illustrated Guide to Worcester Porcelain, 1751–1793*. p. 43. London: Herbert Jenkins.

147. SANDON, H. (1973) *Coffee Pots and Teapots for the Collector*. pp. 29–34. Edinburgh: Bartholomew.

148. SAVAGE, G & NEWMAN, H. (1976) *An Illustrated Dictionary of Ceramics*. p. 286. London: Thames & Hudson.

149. SCHINDLER, A.H. (1896) *Eastern Persian Irak*. pp. 114–116. London: Royal Geographical Society.

150. SELLECK, A.D. (1978) *Cookworthy. 1705–1780*. A man of no common clay, and his circle. pp. 239–241. Plymouth, Devon: Baron Jay. SHAW, K. (1962) *Ceramic Colours and Pottery Decoration*. London: Maclaren.

151. SHAW, S. (1829) *History of the Staffordshire Potteries:* and the Rise and Progress of the Manufacture of Pottery and Porcelain. p. 192. London: Scott, Greenwood edition of 1900.

152. *Ibid*. p. 193.

153. *Ibid*. p. 199.

154. *Ibid*. p. 211.

155. *Ibid*. p. 212.

156. *Ibid*. p. 213.

157. *Ibid.* p. 214.

158. *Ibid.* pp. 215–217.

159. SHAW, S. (1837) *The Chemistry of the Several Natural and Artificial Heterogeneous compounds, used in manufacturing Porcelain, Glass and Pottery.* pp. 314–323. London: The Author.

160. *Ibid.* pp. 515–517.

161. SMITH, A. (1970) *The Illustrated Guide to Liverpool Herculaneum Pottery, 1796–1840.* pp. 191–202. London: Barrie & Jenkins.

162. SMITH, A. (1971) Thomas Wolfe, Miles Mason and John Lucock at the Islington China Manufactory, Upper Islington, Liverpool. et seq. *Trans. Eng. Cer. Cir.* **8** Pt. 2 (1972) p. 199 et seq.

163. SPODE LIMITED MSS (1822–1832) Spode Recipe Books, MSS 797/1.

164. SPODE LIMITED MSS (1833–1856) Copeland & Garrett, and Copeland Recipe Book MSS 906.

165. SPRACKLING, H. (1958) *Customs on the Table Top:* How New England Housewives set out their tables. p. 8. Sturbridge: Mass:

166. STRETTON, H. (1978) The Earthenwares of James Keeling, New Street, Hanley. *c.* 1790–1831. pp. 7–8. London: *Bulletin Morley College Cer. Cir.* **1** No. 1.

167. TAYLOR, J.R. (1977) The Origin and use of Cobalt Compounds as Blue Pigments. *Science and Archeology No. 19.* Stafford.

168. TEMPLEMAN, DR., (1754–1758) Transactions of the Society of Arts **II**, p. 27.

169. *Ibid.* p. 34.

170. *Ibid.* p. 39.

171. *Ibid.* p. 41.

THOMAS, J. (1971) *The Rise of the Staffordshire Potteries.* Bath: Adams & Dart.

TOWNER, D. (1957) *English Cream-Coloured Earthenware.* London: Faber & Faber.

172. TOWNER, D. (1978) *Creamware.* p. 20. London: Faber & Faber.

173. *Ibid.* p. 46.

174. *Ibid.* p. 60.

175. TREVELYAN, G.M. (1944) *English Social History.* pp. 345–348. London: Reprint Society.

176. *Ibid.* pp. 391–392.

177. TUDOR-CRAIG, A. (1928) Chinese Armorial Porcelain. Some Eighteenth-Century Borders. *Antiques* Magazine **XIV**. p. 128.

178. TURNER, W. (1907) *Transfer Printing on Enamels, Porcelain and Pottery,* p. 4 et seq. London: Chapman & Hall.

179. *Ibid.* p. 75.

180. TWINING, S.H. (1956) *The House of Twining,* being a short history of the firm of R. Twining & Co. Ltd. 1706–1956. p. 31. London.

181. *Ibid.* p. 45.

182. *Ibid.* p. 47.

183. URE, A. (1839) *A Dictionary of Arts, Manufactures and Mines:* containing a clear exposition of their principles and practice. p. 932. London.

184. VOLKER, T. (1954) *Porcelain and the Dutch East India Company, 1602–1682.* p. 49. Leiden, Holland: Mededalingen Van Het Rijksmuseum Voor Valkenkunde.

185. *Ibid.* p. 128.

186. VOLKER, T. (1959) *The Japanese Porcelain Trade of the Dutch East India Company after 1683.* Leiden. p. 38. 'merchants in the Southern Netherlands had started trading from Ostend to Canton direct in 1714.'

187. WARD, J. (1843) *The Borough of Stoke-upon-Trent,* comprising its history etc., p. 420. London.

188. WATNEY, B. (1963) *English Blue and White Porcelain of the Eighteenth Century.* p. 8 cites the Society of Arts Register of the Premiums and Bounties, and letters. London: Faber & Faber.

189. *Ibid.* p. 128.

190. WATNEY, B. (1973) *English Blue and White Porcelain of the Eighteenth Century,* p.xviii. London: Faber & Faber.

191. *Ibid.* pp. 47–48.

192. WATSON, J.S. (1960) *The Reign of George III. 1760–1815.* p. 14. Oxford: University Press.

193. WEBB, H.W. (1956) *Cobalt, Nickel and Selenium in Pottery.* pp. 3–17. London: The Mond Nickel Co., (now I.C.I.).

194. WEDGWOOD, J.C. (1913) *Staffordshire Pottery and its History.* p. 67. London.

195. WEDGWOOD MSS. 2200–12.

196. WHITER, L. (1970) *Spode. A History of the Family, Factory and Wares from 1733–1833.* p. 11. London: Barrie & Jenkins.

197. *Ibid.* pp. 30–31.

198. *Ibid.* p. 33.

199. *Ibid.* p. 39.

200. *Ibid.* p. 46.

201. *Ibid.* p. 60.

202. *Ibid.* pp. 70–72.

203. *Ibid.* p. 80.

204. *Ibid.* p. 127.

205. *Ibid.* pp. 141–145.

206. *Ibid.* pp. 188–196.

207. WILLIAMS, C.A.S. (1932) *Outlines of Chinese Symbolism and Art Motives.* An alphabetical compendium of antique legends and beliefs, as reflected in the manners and customs of the Chinese. p. 303. Shanghai: Kelly & Walsh, 2nd Ed.

208. *Ibid.* p. 329.

209. *Ibid.* p. 423–435. Willow Pattern.

210. WILLIAMS, S.B. (1949) *Antique Blue and White Spode.* p. 136. London: Batsford. 3rd Ed.

211. *Ibid.* p. 146.

212. WILLIAMS-WOOD, C. (1976) When Underglaze Printing was a Secret Technique. *Art & Antiques Weekly.* London: Feb. 21st. 1976. pp. 16–19.

YOUNG, R.S. (1948) *Cobalt.* American Chemical Society Monograph No. 108. New York: Reinhold Publishing Corp.

YOUNG, R.S. (   ) *Cobalt. Its Chemistry, Metallurgy, and Uses.* American Chemical Society Monograph Series.

213. YOUNG, W.J. (1949) Discussion of some analyses of Chinese underglaze blue and underglaze red. *Far East Ceramic Bulletin.* **1** (8), 20. p. 22.

INDEX TO PATTERNS

A schedule of the different names given to Spode patterns appears on page 159.